STALKING MICHELANGELO, FINDING GOD

Stalking Michelangelo, Finding God

Christine M. Panyard

RESOURCE *Publications* · Eugene, Oregon

STALKING MICHELANGELO, FINDING GOD

Resource Publications
An Imprint of Wipf and Stock Publishers
199 W. 8th Ave., Suite 3
Eugene, OR 97401

www.wipfandstock.com

PAPERBACK ISBN: 978-1-6667-3949-7
HARDCOVER ISBN: 978-1-6667-3950-3
EBOOK ISBN: 978-1-6667-3951-0

MAY 23, 2022 11:18 AM

Prophet Isaia in the Sistine Chapel, Photo Copyright © Governorate of the Vatican City State-Directorate of the Vatican Museums

To Father James Bilot,

St. Teresa wrote in her autobiography, "The beginner [in spiritual development] requires advice, so that he may see where his greatest benefit lies. To this end a director is most necessary. Therefore, it is very important that the director shall be prudent, I mean a man of sound understanding, and he shall also be experienced. If he has learning as well, that is a great advantage." Thank you for working with this beginner. You've helped me to understand my experience from a spiritual perspective rather than a psychological/scientific one. May you continue to inspirit people for many years to come. Thank you for all you have done for the Lord, His Church and me.

Christine M. Panyard, PhD

"I was content to accept without resistance the stimuli coming from my surroundings, and so, almost without noticing it, became gradually transformed."

ST. EDITH STEIN, *LIFE IN A JEWISH FAMILY*

TABLE OF CONTENTS

LIST OF ILLUSTRATIONS

Acknowledgments

P UBLISHING is a team sport. I would like to thank many people for helping me finish this project. My good friends Nancy Yount, James Rodriguez, and Carol Bussa read the manuscript in the early stages of its development. They offered valuable input from the perspective of an avid reader, an English teacher and a librarian. My brother, James R. Panyard, went back to his roots as a draftsman and produced the floorplan of a gothic cathedral. The Governate of the Vatican City State-Directorate of the Vatican Museums gave me permission to use the image of the Prophet Isaiah from the Sistine Chapel. I would like to thank my project manager, Matt Wimer, and the entire staff of Wipf & Stock Publishers for their faith in this project. They have provided the support and technical expertise necessary to make it a reality.

1

THE JOURNEY BEGINS

"Move along. Move along per favore" barked the tour guide as we were herded through the Vatican Museum. There was no time to admire the wall sized tapestries or the statues from the glory days of the Roman Empire. The museum was crowded with tourists on holiday and students required to contemplate one more work of art. Our group tried to stay together as we were herded through the halls of one of the world's greatest museums towards the most celebrated chapel in Christendom, the Sistine Chapel.

We were funneled into a smallish hallway and through an unpretentious door. I had expected to enter the chapel from the rear and walk towards the altar as you do in most churches. Instead, I found myself at the front of the chapel. Michelangelo's fresco of the *Last Judgment* leapt at me from the right. I could have touched the images of sinners being dragged to hell or ferried over the River Styx by Charon. The most famous chapel in the world exploded with vibrant images I seemed to have known all my life. The paintings on the walls and ceiling were familiar from the huge art books I had left at home, not to mention that they have been used over and over again in our popular culture. God separating light from darkness. God creating the world in a frenzy of energy. Christ separating the saved from the damned. And, of course, the creation of man. God's hand reaching towards Adam to gift him with life is iconic.

I craned my neck to get a better view. It was difficult to navigate the length of the chapel. I wanted to take in as much of the room as possible and not get trampled by other, much taller, tourists. Where would I begin? How could I make sense of the hundreds of figures in the hundreds of paintings that filled the chapel? The noise from the tourists oohing and aahing at this artistic feast and the voices of museum guards yelling "No photo, no photo" produced a cacophony that added to my sense of being overwhelmed. Much too soon, I heard that familiar voice imploring, "Move along. Move along per favore" and we were outside the chapel. My visit to the Sistine Chapel was the highlight of my first trip to Rome. Those twenty minutes with Michelangelo changed my life.

We exited the chapel, turned right through a small hallway and entered St. Peter's Basilica, the grandest church in the world, and designed by Michelangelo. We were at the back of the church and the first chapel we passed held the famous Rome Pieta. Michelangelo sculpted it for the French cardinal Jean de Bilheres. Cardinal Bilheres wanted the most beautiful statue in the world to grace his tomb and he got exactly what he ordered. The Rome Pieta didn't stay with his remains. It was moved many times during the reconstruction of the basilica and now rests safely behind bullet proof glass in a side chapel.

I gasped when I saw the Rome Pieta. Like the paintings on the ceiling of the Sistine Chapel, I was familiar with this work. I didn't expect such a visceral reaction. My heart started to race and Hail Marys started coming out of my mouth like bullets out of a machine gun. I'm a cradle Catholic so saying the familiar prayer was something I've done all my life even when a lapsed Catholic. I've said thousands of Hail Marys when I've been afraid but I never expected them to pour from my lips as I stood before the most beautiful statue in the world. I was touched. I was moved. I was in awe of Michelangelo's ability to capture death and grief in stone. I could see every vein in the feet of Christ and every fold in Mary's gown. The statue seemed capable of movement. Michelangelo, at the tender age of 21, had breathed life into marble.

Michelangelo, so the story goes, overheard someone attributing the Rome Pieta to another sculptor. He snuck into the church at night and carved his name on a sash that crossed the Madonna's chest. "Michelangelo Buonarroti, Florentine made this" is the English translation. His work became so famous and so unique during his lifetime that he never again felt the need to sign any of his sculptures. No artist has ever come close to producing works with the power and detail of Michelangelo. I could have spent more time contemplating the Rome Pieta, but once again I heard "Move along. Move along, per favore."

St. Peter's Basilica, Rome

St. Peter's Basilica is the largest church in the world. As you walk down the central aisle, the nave, you'll find markers of where other cathedrals would fit inside St. Peter's. It is truly one of the most awe-inspiring structures in the world. The architects of the basilica understood the human psyche very well. Everything in the basilica is on a grand scale that makes the individual seem small and humble before God and the Church. The arches and columns are immense. The statues of popes and saints are huge. Everything towers over the visitor as you walk down the nave towards the altar. Above the altar is the dome of St. Peters, the crown jewel in the Roman skyline. No building is allowed to be taller than St. Peter's.

St. Peter's Basilica was more than a thousand years old by the time the Renaissance began. It was dilapidated and in need of replacement. Michelangelo was one of many architects to work on the new basilica. He became the Architect of the Vatican in 1547. He reworked the floor plan and created the dome over the altar. In those days, without the benefit of modern machines to help with construction, raising a building the size of St. Peter's took decades, and in some cases a hundred years. Many architects never lived long enough to see their plans completed. Such was the case with Michelangelo. His student, Giacomo Della Porta, completed the dome of St. Peter's Basilica in 1590, 26 years after Michelangelo died.

The windows in the dome fill the basilica with light. It looks and feels as if divine light is flooding the church. My eyes moved right to the top. There is a gallery around the base of the dome and visitors fit enough can climb the stairs to reach it. Mercifully, signs are posted near the entrance to the dome warning the intrepid pilgrim of the hundreds of steps that await them. I could only imagine what the sight would have been from the gallery. I'm very achievement oriented, a real Type A personality. I was also 56, with one episode of tachycardia under my belt. I decided to heed the voice of my tour guide and "move along".

Interior of St. Peter's Basilica, Rome

My visit to St. Peter's Basilica and the Sistine Chapel left me wanting much more. I wanted more time to explore the collections in the Vatican Museums, more time to pray in this most holy place (Did I really say pray?), and more time to contemplate the works of Michelangelo. In one morning, I saw the most famous frescoes in the world, the most beautiful statue in the world, and the most awesome church in the world. They were all the work of one man. I wanted to understand the roots of Michelangelo's greatness. What artists helped to shaped his work? How did he develop such skill in sculpture, painting and architecture? What was the nature of the faith that sustained him and was the foundation of his work? I was driven to the point of obsession. I wanted to learn all I could about Michelangelo. I was on the brink of a grand adventure as I began stalking Michelangelo.

Michelangelo spent most of his life inside churches or working for the Catholic Church. He was apprenticed as a boy to Dominico Ghirlandaio, a Florentine famous for his frescos. Michelangelo copied the works of his master in his sketchbooks and probably assisted him in churches around town. Michelangelo was a devout Catholic and went to Mass regularly. He knew scripture well and was reported to have memorized quite a bit of Dante's *Divine Comedy*. His conflicts with his papal patrons are legendary and yet he always felt at home in church.

Unlike Michelangelo, I spent a long time outside the Church. I appreciated its role in history, the beauty of its architecture, and the pomp of its rituals but I didn't belong there. Maybe I was too much a product of my culture. Sex, drugs and rock and roll were the creed of a child growing up in the 60's. The old-fashioned virtues of chastity, poverty and obedience didn't seem to apply anymore. The world had moved on. The Church seemed like a relic of a distant era. It didn't fit in the world anymore and I didn't fit in organized religion.

I found myself spending considerable time in churches as I stalked Michelangelo. I wanted to see as much of his work in person as possible and to learn about the artists that influenced him. Seeing an artist's work in person is similar to hearing your favorite singer in concert rather than on the radio or a CD. You can feel the artist's energy when you stand before his work. My growing library of the Renaissance would only take me so far. I needed to go to Europe and spend time in the places that housed, as well as shaped, Michelangelo's work. I needed to see the art in the places for which it was created. My passion for Michelangelo's art took me to London, Paris, St. Petersburg, Rome, Florence, Sienna, Bologna, and Carrara. Many people use Fodor's or Rick Steve's books as travel guides. I used William Wallace's *Michelangelo-Sculpture, Painting, Architecture.* My spring breaks and summer vacations were spent visiting churches and museums around the world. When I exhausted my supply of friends willing to follow my itinerary, I started going by myself. I know it's weird for a sixty-something to take off for Europe by herself, but that's what I did. I amassed a huge collection of books and photographs of churches. Then I started having crazy, strange experiences in churches.

A passion for Michelangelo and Renaissance art led me back to church. I was reading about the artists and architects who made that time so special and spending countless hours in museums and churches. Professor William R. Cook wrote, "A Gothic cathedral is an expression of the basic truths of Christianity and the values, hopes, and worldly desires of the people who built them." The architecture, paintings, stained glass and statues that surrounded me were a physical representation of the teachings of the Catholic Church. I wasn't aware of how being in churches, the house of God, was changing me. St. Edith Stein wrote in *Life in a Jewish Family,* "I was content to accept without resistance the stimuli coming from my surroundings, and so, almost without noticing it, became gradually transformed." It happened so slowly. I didn't see or feel it working in my soul. I thought I was learning about art. Actually, the churches and cathedrals that surrounded me transformed me. I walked through the front door of countless churches and cathedrals spiritually as well as physically and have been moving towards the altar ever since.

2

Looking Back

I was never very religious. I was raised Roman Catholic but wouldn't say that I was raised in a very Catholic home. My parents sent my brother and me to Catechism until the 8th grade. We were given the choice to attend or not after that. We chose "or not." They made us go to Mass on Sundays, but didn't take us to church after they were certain we could make it on our own. That must have been very early because I don't remember ever going with my parents. In the "olden days" it was safe to send your first and second graders down the street to school or to church. There was never a doubt that we would come home safely and we always did.

My brother and I continued going to Mass until we were young adults, more out of habit than piety. I always checked the box Roman Catholic on survey and census forms. There should have been space to write lukewarm or lapsed to be more accurate. My involvement in the liturgy was superficial and I wasn't involved in the church at all beyond going to the sock hops at St. Christopher. I walked away from the Church as a young adult and stayed away from church for 15 years. I became a lapsed Catholic, a member of one of the world's largest denominations.

There was no single event that made me leave. I didn't experience a crisis in faith or a conflict with a particular priest. I simply didn't need it. I decided not to follow the rules, including the Ten Commandments, and the regulations that had worked pretty well for more than two thousand years. I was above all that stuff. I described myself as spiritual, but not religious, a real cop-out. To most that means that you can say you are connected to

God without having a covenantal relationship with God. You make up the rules and morality as you go along. You do your own thing rather than follow His laws.

I had succumbed to the spirit of the 60's and 70's. Challenge the establishment. If it feels good, do it. The Second Vatican Council, convened by Pope John XXIII, was making sweeping changes in the Catholic Church. The fundamental beliefs and tenants remained the same, but the form changed dramatically. Gone were services in Latin and the incense at High Mass on Sundays. Gone were the statues of saints. People were taking Communion in their own hands and receiving it every Sunday. We were singing hymns like Protestants. Rectories, convents and churches were emptying at an alarming rate.

One day I found myself in my old neighborhood. I don't remember what I was doing there. I could have been there on business or shopping at one of the Polish bakeries in the area. My childhood parish was close by so I decided to stop in for no particular reason. It wasn't a holy day. There wasn't anything I wanted to pray for. I just wanted to see the old place. I sat alone in the empty church. I enjoyed seeing the familiar statues and the smell of years of incense and candle smoke. It was familiar and very comfortable. Then I started to cry. What a strange thing to do and what a surprise. I would have described myself as very happy. My life was going well. I was succeeding at my career, living well on my own, and involved with an exciting new man. So why was I crying? I dried my tears, checked my make-up, and left. I know now that my soul was sad that I was going away. I don't remember sharing that experience with anyone or stopping in a church for anything other than a wedding or funeral for a long, long time.

About 15 years later I started going to Mass again. The church of Christ the King was just a few blocks from my home and I usually walked, something Detroiters rarely do. One Sunday I sat next to two of the few people I knew in the parish. I was crying by the Our Father. I had been married for a few years. My husband was a twice-divorced man, which as far as the Church was concerned, made it a fornicated relationship. Why was this thing happening again? I learned many years later that it was the Gift of Tears, an encounter with the Holy Spirit. My exile from the Church had been bookended by the Gift of Tears. I had no idea how many times I would encounter the Holy Spirit or how many blessings I would receive over the next thirty years. I wouldn't even recognize my experiences as blessings.

I just thought of them as the way the world was, or most often, as a bit strange and bizarre.

I was much too busy to explore my spiritual life. I worked and worked and worked: 50 hours a week as a psychologist, 20 hours a week training German Shepherd Dogs, and God knows how many hours running a household. My husband was a lapsed non-denominational Christian and not supportive of my return to church. When I described the generosity of my parish, he would rag on the pope and complain about my small offering. If I returned home five minutes later than usual, he thought I was having an affair. In a way he was right. I was beginning a relationship with Jesus. Jesus knocked on my door for over forty years before I heard Him. I finally opened the door and walked into the house of the Lord. I was returning to my spiritual home. I am so grateful that He had patience and didn't give up on me. He let me come home.

3

OUT OF A RUT AND INTO
A NEW LIFE

N ATIONAL Geographic magazines filled our home when I was a child.
I looked forward to every new issue and the chance to explore the
world, if only from our living room. I hoped that I would travel to those
exiting places and visit those beautiful churches and palaces someday, too.
My adventures waited until I had finished school. I spent 10 years as a full-
time college student, so they waited a long time. When I finished my doc-
torate in counseling at Wayne State University, I took myself to Greece as
a graduation present. Eventually I climbed the pyramids of the Egyptians,
lounged on the beach in Tahiti and definitely did not break the bank in
Monte Carlo. My work with substance abusers and police officers, a very
interesting clientele, took me to workshops, seminars and professional
conferences around the United States. My wandering stopped when I got
married. Oh, we went on vacations, but they were motorcycle trips to Cape
Cod or fishing and hunting trips to northern Michigan. I didn't go further
abroad than Toronto during the thirteen years I was married. They were
great experiences, but I missed the inspiration found traveling abroad.

The first six or seven years of marriage were pretty good, the last six or
seven weren't. Women give up a lot to be married and I was no exception.
Of course, I was a child of the 60's and expected that my marriage would be
different. All that stuff about the man needing to be older, taller, smarter,
better educated, have a higher status job and make more money was only

a social construction to many women at that time. However, research on marital satisfaction has found those things to be important predictors of success. I hadn't read the research so I married a police officer who was fun to play with. Play was important. I had spent most of my youth in the library working on a Ph.D. By the time I was 28, I was the director of a multimillion-dollar grant that provided services to over three thousand substance abusers annually. It seems as if I've always been an adult. So being able to play was very attractive. A couple needs to be able to manage the business aspects of a marriage as well as play-time. We weren't very good at that.

Our marriage lacked reciprocity. Like many couples, the money I earned became "our" money. But the money he earned was his. We were in a fortunate position of being able to afford just about anything we wanted, just not everything and my husband wanted everything. I thought that if he got a new car, refurbished his motorcycle and bought every fishing lure in Cabela's that he would be happy. Of course, he wasn't. Less and less of our resources were available for me. I worked very hard as a psychologist. My private practice and consulting business boomed and I was promoted at the university. I couldn't make money fast enough for him and I began to resent him. "But you don't want anything" he would say. My lists that included travel abroad and good china were ignored. Heaven forbid I should bring up planning for retirement. He gave no thought to what we would need in the future, only what he wanted now.

This lack of reciprocity carried over to our leisure activities as well. I thought that if I dragged deer out of the woods and helped process them that my husband would go to the ballet and the Detroit Institute of Arts with me. No. It didn't work that way. I went to the ballet with my girlfriends and stopped going to the DIA. My husband was a great companion if you were playing his games, but he didn't think it was necessary to play mine. He was capable of parallel play, but not interactive play and all he did was play. While he sighted his bow or rebuilt his motorcycle trailer for the nine hundredth time, I mowed three acres of lawn and painted the basement. I tried to think of cutting the grass as meditation on a John Deer, but it didn't work. I wanted to play, too. I wanted to spend my free time doing more than home maintenance. I wanted to play my games, not just his.

My husband would probably say otherwise, but I tried very hard to be a supportive wife. My parents were married for over fifty years and enjoyed each other until the day my mother died. They both worked hard to make our family successful. I expected that marriage would be work, that it would involve give and take. So, I gave and gave and felt that I took very little back. I took care of household maintenance inside and out. I made most of the money and paid the bills. I did the laundry, the cooking, grocery shopping and spent a lot of time with his daughters. I mowed parking lots for motorcycle events and cooked for the hungry crowds. Marriage wore me out. I couldn't live in a dirty house or not pay the bills, so I gave up sex. As much as I always liked it, sex was something I could live without and one thing I could refuse to contribute to the household. As so often happens, the very thing that I found attractive, his playfulness, drove us apart. I needed a helpmate as well as a playmate. He didn't support me in any way. He even refused to accompany me to funerals. I'm a weeper, so my friends and relatives comforted me rather than my husband. Pretty soon there was nothing left but anger and resentment.

Our German Shepherd Samson had an interesting way of managing our arguments. Whenever we raised our voices, Sam would come over and sit on my lap. When we calmed down, he would go back to wherever he was enjoying a nap. He never growled or barked. He just sat his 110 pounds on my lap. I never knew whether he was protecting me from my husband or my husband from me.

Anger is corrosive. I know that. I'm a psychologist. So, my blood pressure increased along with my weight. I didn't want to come home. I didn't want to look at my husband and I grew to hate the smell of his clothes. We had different work schedules. He worked 6:00 am to 2:00 pm and I worked 10:00 am to 8:00 pm. I dreaded coming home to a sad eyed man asking, "What's for dinner?" Often, I would feign a lack of appetite and settle for a bowl of cereal. I knew that I could not continue this way.

There is always a straw that breaks the camel's back. It's the same in marriage. It's rarely one thing that destroys the bond, but an accumulation of hurts and disappointments. My straw came in the form of a $5000 check my husband received from the Police Protection and Benefit Association for reaching his 25th anniversary with the department. After spending $10,000 on toys for himself in one year, he was complaining that we didn't have the same amount in savings to invest as a down payment on his next car that we had for mine several years before. Of course, we didn't. If you buy an ATV, a computer and surveillance cameras, you aren't going to have the money for a car. All the time he complained, he had the check for $5000 in his pocket. I worked with police officers and knew more about his department than he did. I knew the check was coming. He couldn't lie to me like other officers have been known to do to their wives. When he asked me what I wanted to do about insurance for the new car, I said, "What I really want to do is get divorced."

I took half the money from our accounts, put it in a safe place, and called an attorney. In four months, we were divorced. It was very civilized. I kept what I paid for and the dogs. It was a surreal experience to stand before the judge and declare that the marriage was over. In less than ten minutes, an important chapter in my life, one that lasted thirteen years, was over. My soon to be ex-husband showed up in court and wanted one more explanation of why I left. The simplest reason is that I was losing myself. If I didn't leave, I would cease to exist.

All cultures celebrate milestones with feasts and celebrations. Births, graduations, weddings, retirements and deaths bring families together to share the experience. We rejoice and grieve together. We laugh and cry and share food to mark these events. But we get divorced alone. We don't yet have a ritual for sharing this milestone. It was very difficult for me to fail at something as important as marriage. I left the courthouse and comforted myself with a super- sized order of apple pancakes. Alone.

Divorce changes not only your marital status, but your social network as well. I had been part of a couple for many years and you are treated very differently as part of a couple than as a divorced woman. The friendships we shared ended and my social life changed drastically. My cousin Nena was divorced shortly after me. Her thirty-year marriage ended when her husband ran off with another woman. Our family is probably strange. You can divorce a Panyard, but you can never leave the Panyard family. So, we still see Nena's husband at family events just like we do cousin Bill's ex-wife and my brother's first wife. One of the first things we did after our divorces was to renew our passports. Nena and I became traveling buddies for the next few years. We were both ready to explore the world again. I knew that at my age, 47, the odds of getting remarried were slim. In addition to being too old, I felt that I was probably too intense, too independent and too successful to be wife material. It would be easy to find someone older and taller than me, but smarter, better educated, with a higher status position and at least as much money as I made would be highly unlikely. Those kinds of men want women twenty years their junior, not a fascinating, passionate middle-aged woman. So, I was very happy to have my cousin become my new best friend. I had a pent-up desire to travel and I hit the ground running. With the ink barely dried on our new passports, Nena and I headed for China. I've been on the road ever since.

My fifties were the most difficult years of my life. A lot is written about how hard it is to be a teenager, but adolescence is nothing compared to menopause. There are no easy lives and there is no easy way to get through menopause. In addition to recovering from divorce, I found myself struggling to reclaim my body. I was lucky in that I did not have those awful sweats or mood swings. What I had was an unending period. That's a funny way to put it. A period signals the end of something, a sentence or a historical age. My period could only be described as torrential and it was always raining. My gynecologist assured me that we could correct the problem with surgery or simply wait until nature took its course. When my ovaries stopped working, my fibroid tumor, which was the size of an orange, would shrink and I would have no further problem. I decided to let nature take its course and was anemic for the next five years.

I'm a small person. I never made it to five feet tall and I had been able to keep my weight pretty well under control. During my fifties middle age spread made a dramatic appearance. My thighs were no longer a problem. All my extra fat miraculously moved to my back. I was developing wings, those dreaded flaps opposite the bicep that don't seem to respond to exercise. No more tank tops or sleeveless cocktail dresses for me. And my face. I was melting. My eyelids drooped. My jaw line sagged and I was developing a waddle any turkey would have been proud to claim. I didn't look like Chris Panyard. Where was that cheerleader who used to peer back from the mirror?

Then my friends and relatives started dying off at an alarming rate. My best friend at the University died the same month my divorce was final. I was a basket case. I cried for three days and was unable to teach and nothing keeps me from my classroom. My seven-month-old German Shepherd wouldn't leave my side. He even slept with me, which was unusual. For those three days, every time I woke, I would find his paw or head on me. He knew I needed to be comforted and was much more useful than my ex-husband. I lost four cousins in a six-month period and went to twelve funerals in one year. It seemed like everyone from my secretary's baby to my 105-year-old aunt was checking out. My mother and two of her cousins died within two weeks. No sooner did I start to recover from one death then someone else died. I was exhausted from the unending grief. I was tired all the time.

Chris Panyard is a trooper. I am a Type A personality and probably border on hypomanic. Certainly, thinking that someone would actually want to read my story is a bit grandiose! Having much more energy than the average person, I had tremendous reserves from which to draw. So, I kept taking care of business. I met all my responsibilities at the University and with my consulting business. My home never looked better. The money that had been spent on hunting and fishing trips was now spent on redecorating and good china. I still did all the cleaning, landscaping and financial management. I found it much easier to do everything by myself when I lived alone rather than when I had a husband. Anger and resentment towards him made everything more difficult. I maintained a busy training schedule in the wacky sport of Schutzhund. I was teaching my dog to perform in tracking, obedience and protection competitions. It looks a lot like working a police dog, but it is for sport. We collect ribbons and trophies, rather than bad guys. I even made it to the national championships in 2000. And I still managed to spend time with friends and family. If I hadn't been hypomanic to begin with, I probably would have collapsed. My hectic lifestyle kept me from recognizing that I was mildly depressed for most of my fifties. Of course, I remained untreated and alone.

I made several attempts to reconnect with men. There was the accountant who seemed to be a perfect match – bright, successful, educated at my university and a practicing Catholic. After staying with him for a week in San Diego, I discovered that he really drank way too much for my comfort and he discovered that he really wasn't attracted to me after all. Then there was the history professor. Our lunches off campus felt like dates, not just a meal with a colleague. When he found out I was nine years his senior, the lunches ended. I was attracted to other men but they were either married or gay which, in either case, doomed the relationships. I was really terrified of a connection, terrified that I would give up too much of myself in the process, afraid that I would lose Chris Panyard again.

My fifties were such a struggle. I was recovering from the failure of my marriage, my body was betraying me, too many people in my life were dying and I did not have a special person to love me. So, I began to travel. I went to Las Vegas several times, went on tour with the Southwest Indian Foundation, joined the throngs walking across the Mackinaw Bridge in northern Michigan on Labor Day, and went to China with Nena. Unfortunately for me, Nena found the love of her life and her second husband at Single Point, a singles group for middle aged folks at her church. I gained a cousin-in-law and lost a travel buddy. Mary, another psychology professor, joined us in Las Vegas and continued to travel with me. Before long, we headed for Italy.

It took a long time for me to get to Rome. That's kind of strange for someone who loves art and ancient civilizations. Little did I know, how much that adventure would change my life. Ancient Rome was the theme of our first day. We trekked through the Forum and the Coliseum and I imagined listening to Roman orators and witnessing gladiators in action. We spent the next day in Christian Rome. We visited the catacombs and the major basilicas, St. John Lateran, St. Paul Outside the Walls, and St. Mary Major. That left us with an afternoon at the Vatican. It was a whirlwind tour to say the least.

We marched through the Vatican Museum to the sound of the tour guide barking "Move along, move along per favore." There was no time to stop and admire anything, let alone contemplate what we passed on our way to the Sistine Chapel. I wanted more time to appreciate such magnificent work and to understand what it all meant. I knew I would be back but had no idea what an important part in my life Michelangelo would play.

Getting back into my daily routine was easy and life went along much like before that fateful trip to Rome. Once in a while I would pick up a book about Renaissance art or see an exhibit at the Detroit Institute of Arts. A colleague of mine at the University of Detroit Mercy recommended *The Pope's Ceiling*, an interesting read about the painting of the Sistine Chapel. Before long my interest in Michelangelo and Renaissance art became an obsession. I started stalking Michelangelo.

I went to Italy seven times and France three times in an attempt to learn more about Michelangelo's work and the roots of his greatness. I amassed a huge library of the Renaissance and took a dozen video and audio courses from the Teaching Company on my new passion, religious art. Roma Downey, star of *Touched by an Angel*, and her husband Mark Burnett, the producer of *The Survivor* and *The Apprentice*, produced the acclaimed television series *The Bible, AD,* and the movie *The Son of God.* She quoted Kevin Gould in an interview that "God doesn't always call the qualified, but he always qualifies the called." It seemed as if God was qualifying me for my next career through travel and my passion for Renaissance art.

I searched for a book that brought together Michelangelo's paintings in the Sistine Chapel with the scripture on which they were based. It seemed strange that no one had done such a thing in the 500 years since he first laid brush to ceiling. So, I did it. I wasn't qualified to pursue such a project. My religious education ended in the 8th grade and I never took a college course in art history. Apparently, God called me to do this work and qualified me with what has become a lifetime of independent study. I signed a contract with Paulist Press to publish *The Sistine Chapel a Biblical Tour* in 2008, exactly five hundred years after Michelangelo signed his contract with Pope Julius II to paint the Sistine Chapel. He took four years to complete the job. It took five years for my book to see the light of day. Wonder of wonders, not only was *The Sistine Chapel a Biblical Tour* published by Paulist Press, the largest Catholic publishing house in America, the Libreria Editrice Vaticana released an Italian edition.

How could such a thing happen? How could a psychologist who specialized in heroin addicts and police officers publish a book about Michelangelo and Scripture? How could she get the Vatican to publish her first book in Italian? I can only explain it as having been moved by the Holy Spirit and I know that sounds crazy. No dove or tongue of fire appeared in my home. Michelangelo didn't tap me on the shoulder during one of my visits and say he wanted me to work with him. Somehow, I was slowly and with purpose moved to do this work. I called it my crazy work for a long time until one of my cousins said it wasn't crazy work, it was my new work. I was through with the problems and perversions of patients in psychological pain. I was moved to work with beauty and spirit and to share it with others.

In the course of my new work, I visited churches all over the world and spent time in countless museums. It changed me in ways I didn't see coming. There was no "come to Jesus" moment when I heard the voice of God, was hit by a thunderbolt or saw spirits. Spending so much time in churches, from the cave churches of the early Christians in Turkey to the Baroque splendor of the Vatican, was bound to have an impact on my psyche. It would be unrealistic to expect to immerse oneself in the study of beauty and spirit and not be changed.

Catholic churches differ from churches of other Christian denominations. People are quieter, more reverential. Catholic churches differ in that we believe they house the presence of God. The doctrine of transubstantiation holds that when the bread and wine are consecrated at Mass, they become the actual body, blood, soul and divinity of Jesus Christ. The Holy Eucharist does not represent or symbolize Christ's blessing of bread at the Last Supper. It becomes His body and blood. The Holy Eucharist is kept in the tabernacle, a beautiful structure on the altar or in a side chapel. The tabernacle corresponds to the Holy of Holies in the temples of the Old Testament. Christ's presence is indicated by a red light. It might be a candle, an oil lamp or an electric light and it is always lit when the Blessed Sacrament is present. God is everywhere. However, He is manifested physically in the Holy Eucharist kept in the tabernacle. His physical presence is what makes Catholic churches feel special. Catholic churches are more than gathering places. They feel like holy places.

Many Catholics receive the Holy Eucharist every time they come to Mass, every Sunday or daily. Consuming Holy Communion is as close as one can get to God. The Holy Eucharist draws people to Christ. It's not like some kind of laser or tractor beam. If you spend time in the presence of the Holy Eucharist, it will draw you closer to God. That's just how it works. I spent hundreds of hours in Catholic churches while I stalked Michelangelo and studied Renaissance art. I spent hundreds of hours in the presence of the Blessed Sacrament and Christ drew me to himself.

I had many quiet mystical experiences along the way. I thought they were weird or crazy so I sought out the advice of a spiritual director. He assured me that I was not psychotic. He said I had been showered with blessings. I came to think that the Holy Spirit had touched me. I used to put people who talked like that on medication or in a hospital. I wasn't delusional and I wasn't hallucinating. I was being moved to a different kind of life.

If you are part of western civilization, you know much more about churches than you think. You can even take a quiz on Facebook to see how Catholic or Jewish you really are. Non-Catholics and even non-Christians might find themselves in church from time to time. You might have been in one to attend the wedding of a friend or a funeral of a colleague. You might have visited a local church for musical performances, community meetings, or support groups. It would be hard to find a city or town in the Americas or Europe that does not have a church as a center of activity. When you travel, cathedrals are frequently part of the itinerary. College general education requirements expose you to churches and the Church in history, political science, and art courses. The focus of the classes may not be religious, but they can't be taught without a nod to Christianity.

Dan Brown introduced millions of moviegoers and readers to the glorious churches in Italy and Great Britain. After the success of *The Da Vinci Code*, tours were offered with the purpose of visiting the sites portrayed in

Brown's fiction. Even if you are a secular news junkie, you can't miss the stories coming out of the Vatican or the war on Christians and churches in the Middle East. You would be surprised how much you have learned through exposure and osmosis. Churches tell us about the growth of western civilization, the histories of our greatest cities, and, for many of us, the stories of our own families.

I have been on the road for a long time and have taken thousands of photographs and amassed a considerable collection of books from churches around the world. I wanted to do something with them. I learned so much about art, history, architecture, culture, and faith. I have been moved to tell you my story in words and pictures. Much more than a travelogue, I hope to share how being in churches changed me. Be careful. You might change, too.

4

STUDYING ART AS
A FAITH JOURNEY

I was a professor. I studied for a living. So, it would not surprise anyone to learn that I have a lot of books, thousands of books. I studied all facets of psychology as I prepared lectures and wrote professional papers. I turned my research skills in earnest to Renaissance art and religion. By 2010, I had purchased 175 books, listened to 28 Great Courses on CDs, and learned "italiano touristico" with the help of Rosetta Stone. Only a dozen of those books remains on my shelves unread. I'll get to them eventually. Despite my insatiable appetite for knowledge about the Renaissance, I continued to fulfill all of my responsibilities at the University and with my police departments. My house stayed clean and I had a social life. I didn't become a recluse while I became an expert in this new field. Mania helps.

By now I had read a number of biographies of Michelangelo as well as works about the Vatican frescoes and the restoration of his work. I had a good understanding of how he came to paint the ceiling, but not a good understanding of the theology behind the paintings. It is a myth that Michelangelo was a grizzled old man who worked alone on the ceiling of the Sistine Chapel. He was only 33 years old when he began the project. The ceiling covered 5,700 square feet and would have been impossible for one person, even someone as talented as Michelangelo, to do alone. In reality, he had a crew of thirteen painters and assistants to help.

We don't know exactly who was involved in the design of the ceiling, but it would be a mistake to assume that Michelangelo was given permission to paint as he pleased. Renaissance artists were craftsmen who worked at the pleasure of their patrons. They were not free spirits who worked on their projects and hoped to find customers for their work like artists today. The Pope's theologians, Cardinal Alidosi and prior general of the Augustinian Order, Egidio Antonini were probably involved in the design of the ceiling.

The grand scheme of the ceiling of the Sistine Chapel included nine stories from the Book of Genesis, four stories of the redemption of the Jewish people, twelve prophets and sibyls who foretold the coming of Christ, twenty-four paintings of the ancestors of Christ, and twenty male nudes holding ten medallions representing stories from the Old Testament. I was familiar with many of the stories from popular songs and readings in church. We sang of "those bone, those bones, those dry bones" in elementary school and George Gershwin told of "old Jonah who lived in a whale" in Porgy and Bess. I learned about the story of creation and the fall of man in catechism classes. But I didn't have any idea about the Bronze Serpent or Elisha Curing Naaman of Leprosy. And sibyls. What were sibyls, female prophets from antiquity, doing in a Catholic church? I found my copy of the New American Bible and began to read.

Prior to Vatican II, Catholics didn't read the Bible much. In all fairness, for the first 1500 years of the Church, bibles were not available to most people. The only copies that existed were those laboriously copied by hand in monasteries. Those were too expensive for most people to afford even if they could read. Catholics heard excerpts from the Bible in church each Sunday. Those excerpts, the epistles and gospels, were followed by a homily that explained the passages for that day. It's horrible to admit, but even as a kid I didn't pay much attention to those homilies. Most of the Bible study sessions I did attend were recitation and reflection by people who didn't know anything about it. As an educator and someone who is widely read, I often wound up explaining how the passage came to be written and what the author probably meant. I even found myself up at the blackboard drawing Venn diagrams of the Holy Trinity. Believe me, it was neither useful nor satisfying. Now I had a purpose in reading the Bible. I wanted to understand the meaning behind Michelangelo's beautiful frescoes.

As I began my study of the biblical basis of Michelangelo's work, I started to participate more in the faith formation activities at my church.

I went to a workshop on Etty Hillesum. Her diary is an adult version of Anne Frank. I walked on a canvas reproduction of the labyrinth in Chartres Cathedral in our activities center and I attended church more often. My life seemed to run more smoothly when I went to church on a regular basis. It might have been the calming effects of participating in the familiar ritual of the Mass. Maybe it pleased God to see me there and so he was nicer to me. I was hardly "born again" when I started stalking Michelangelo.

I continued to read scholarly works as well as the Bible. I was familiar with Ross King, William Wallace and John Addington Symonds. I couldn't find a book that brought together Michelangelo's beautiful paintings in the Sistine Chapel with the scripture on which they were based. She who had never taken a course in either biblical studies or art history decided to write one. What a crazy thing to do! I didn't have any experience or the credentials to attack such a project. I was a psychologist. I worked with pain and perversion, not beauty and spirit. I worked with heroin addicts and police officers. If you had post-traumatic stress disorder or a problem with substance abuse, I was the one to see, but certainly not the person you sought out for spiritual guidance or for an opinion on Renaissance art.

I earned a minor in history a hundred years ago when I was an undergraduate student at Wayne State University, but I didn't have any training in historical methods. My religious education stopped when I was thirteen. My art education consisted of a yearly trip to the Detroit Institute of Arts and looking at the paintings at Federal's Department Store with my father. Was I going crazy? Was I having a manic episode? I wasn't sure so I kept quiet about my passion for Michelangelo and scripture.

Creating a book about Michelangelo and scripture wasn't that difficult. It surprised me to find that no one else had done it in the hundreds of years since Michelangelo completed the ceiling. I had a sizeable collection of books about him and I had a Bible. I started to scan pictures from my scholarly textbooks into my computer and to type out passages from the Bible. With the diligent use of cut and paste, and no concern for copywrite infringement, I began my first draft of *The Sistine Chapel A Biblical Tour*. It was an exciting process. I was in the flow. I would work for hours. I would get hungry at four o'clock in the afternoon and remember that I hadn't stopped for lunch. Writing psychological reports or articles for professional journals never did that for me. I was feeling excited, creative and spiritually alive.

Many museums have great collections of Renaissance art, but the best places to study that genre are cathedrals. Religious institutions have always commissioned a significant amount of art. Churches, temples, mosques and burial monuments are included in almost every tourist itinerary and provide insight into the values and daily lives of their creators. The art aficionado better appreciates art and its purpose when he sees it in the place for which it was designed.

I began my study of art in Rome and soon found myself visiting the cave churches of the earliest Christians in Turkey, Byzantine churches in Istanbul and Romanesque and Gothic cathedrals throughout Europe. I went on pilgrimages in the United States and Canada and the Holy Land. I zigzagged across countries and time periods. My way to the Lord was anything but straight. My travels were haphazard. I wanted to learn more about art, but didn't do it in a systematic manner. If a tour looked good and fit my academic calendar, I went. Presenting my spiritual journey is difficult because, for the most part, I didn't know I was on one. The more time I spent in churches, the closer I felt to God. It sounds very logical, but was a tremendous surprise to me.

5

EARLY CHRISTIAN CHURCHES

C HURCHES come in many sizes and shapes. The earliest Christian
services were probably conducted in the believers' homes. The first
Christians were people of modest means. Their homes would have been
simple structures that could never have survived until today. We can
only imagine what it would be like to worship with the early Christians.
Members would re-enact the Last Supper when Jesus celebrated the
Passover Feast with his apostles. There were probably people at those first
Masses who knew the apostles and may have heard Jesus preaching in the
Temple or in Galilee. The group may have contained people who witnessed
the Crucifixion. It would have been a warm and intimate experience.

Emperor Constantine legalized Christianity in 313 AD. Freed from
the persecution of the Roman Empire, at least temporarily, Christianity
spread throughout the Mediterranean and worship spaces changed with
the technology, terrain and resources of the regions. Turkey is a treasure
trove of early Christian churches.

Cappadocia is in the central region of Turkey known as Anatolia. The
awesome landscape was formed from lava flows laid down millions of years
ago. Wind, rain and ice sculpted the fairy chimneys we see today. The stone
was soft and the earliest inhabitants were able to carve homes and even cit-
ies above and below the surface of the ground. Churches and monasteries
were carved into the stone when Christianity came to this region. They pro-
vided safe, durable and defensible structures when the Muslims moved in
during the 7th century. The churches were built either high above ground

or deep below the surface. They were very difficult to enter but provided a safe place for worship. Monks lived in many of the structures and people from the surrounding community came for services and sacraments.

The terrain was harsh and unforgiving. I was glad we came in an air-conditioned bus rather than on a donkey or camel. We were a small group of professors and administrators from the University of Detroit Mercy. The Niagara Foundation, a Turkish American organization dedicated to improving inter-faith and inter-national relationships, sponsored us. Even though we were at important sites of early Christianity and most of us were Catholic, this was a tour and not a pilgrimage. We were there to see the sites and learn about the people and culture of the region. It was a very academic approach to Cappadocia. There was no time to linger in the cave churches, contemplate the life of early Christians or pray. Tour guides all over the world want to keep us moving, not praying.

Ephesus came to be my favorite place in Turkey. I knew of Ephesus from the letters of St. Paul to the Ephesians in the New Testament. It was an important seaport to Cimmerians, Persians, Greeks, and Romans. Ephesus was important for the dissemination of ideas as well as goods. It's not surprising that it would be such an important site in the dissemination of the Good News, the Gospel.

According to John 19:26-27 Jesus said to his mother from the cross "Woman, there is your son. In turn he said to the disciple (John, the one he loved) 'There is your mother.' From that hour onward, the disciple took her into his care." We don't have any documentation about Mary after her son was crucified. The Church teaches that she was assumed into heaven. Her body was not corrupted by death. It was taken directly to heaven just like her son's body ascended into heaven. However, there is documentation about St. John and his move to Ephesus. It is assumed that Mary went with him.

Cappadocian Cave Church, Turkey

Mary's home in Ephesus had a mystical discovery. Sr. Katarina Emmerich, who had been bedridden for 12 years, had visions of the home and gave detailed descriptions of the structure. A research team went to the area in 1891 and found the structure described by Sr. Katarina. The foundation was from the first century. Even though there is no hard and fast proof that Mary lived there, the site has become a religious shrine to both Christians and Muslims. I was surprised to learn that Muslims venerate Mary and even allocate one book in the Koran to the mother of Christ. A church sits on the foundation today. Pilgrims can drink water from a fountain outside the church that is said to have health-giving properties. I filled my water bottle at the fountain ready to take advantage of any special gifts it might contain. We were hurried through Ephesus and I felt a loss. I felt the loss of time I could have spent with Our Blessed Mother, Mary.

Back in Istanbul we visited the most famous of all Byzantine churches, the Haghia Sophia, Holy Wisdom. Roman Emperor Justinian built it in 532. The soaring dome seems to float as it rests on a series of arches. It is a massive and imposing structure. The inside was filled with mosaics made with ground gold. The gold and light from the dome made the interior dazzle. It was converted into a mosque under the Ottoman Empire. The Christian mosaics and frescoes were covered with plaster and whitewash. Haghia Sophia was turned into a secular museum in 1935. The ancient Christian art was discovered during the restoration. It is ironic that Muslims protected the Christian art when they attempted to obliterate it. Byzantine art spread around the Mediterranean world and presents, not so subtly, the majesty and omnipotence of God.

Haghia Sophia, Istanbul, Turkey

6

STIRRING IN MY SOUL

I LOVED visiting the early Christian churches. They appealed to the old historian lurking in me. I didn't experience any special feelings in them. Maybe it was because we ran through them so quickly. Maybe it was that I approached them as a tourist and not a pilgrim. A tourist and a pilgrim might cover the same territory, but they do it very differently. The tourist is interested in seeing as much as possible, taking as many pictures as possible and buying as many souvenirs as possible. The tourist wants to get his money's worth. The pilgrim approaches the sites in a prayerful manner. Rather than running through churches, the pilgrim stays to pray. Mass, scripture readings and other devotional acts are written into the itinerary. Pilgrims are actually expected to spend time with God and let God determine what they are to receive. Even though the early churches fascinated me, they didn't stir my soul. I didn't feel anything even close to religious, let alone mystical, in those churches.

I didn't encounter God until I started hanging out in Romanesque, Gothic and Renaissance churches. The major difference between these churches and the early Christian churches was that the Romanesque, Gothic and Renaissance churches were still in use as Catholic churches. They were not empty relics of the past. They hadn't been turned into museums or tourist sites. They had active congregations and busy worship schedules. Prayer services, the sacraments and the Mass were still being celebrated in those buildings. The Holy Eucharist was still present in their tabernacles. I was in the physical presence of Christ in a way that wasn't possible in the early Christian churches. The physical presence of Christ in the Holy Eucharist had a profound effect on me.

Romanesque churches were built during the Middle Ages from approximately 800 -1140 AD. The name comes from the fact that their architectural style is similar to that of the Romans. Both used rounded arches and pillars to carry the weight of the roofs. Wooden roofs were subject to fire damage. There was no fire retardant lumber available and the fire departments consisted of bucket brigades from undependable wells. Stone roofs were very durable and very heavy. The weight would create tremendous pressure on the walls, pushing them outward and causing the building to collapse. Builders created very thick walls with very small windows to withstand that force and they could only build so high. Romanesque churches are dark and cool, cave-like. The soaring Gothic cathedrals with glorious stained-glass windows would need to wait for future architectural developments.

I went to Carrara, Italy to see the marble fields where Michelangelo quarried his stone. He wrote that he enjoyed his time in Carrara immensely and I wanted to see where he worked. I wanted to touch the raw materials he used and breathe the mountain air that inspired and refreshed him. I also wanted to see where he worshiped. I found the small Romanesque church where he heard Mass in an older, working class neighborhod. The church was decorated for a wedding. White bouquets perched on the ends of the pews and flowers lined the area behind the altar. The only other person in the church was the organist. When I sat down, he began to play. It felt like a private concert and I revelled in my good fortune. How lucky was that! I arrived in Michelangelo's church, decorated for a wedding and in time to hear the organist perform!

My pursuit of Michelangelo took me to Florence. After all, it was his home town and he spent his formative years there. He lived with Lorenzo de Medici and was exposed to the best of Renaissance thought and culture. He sat at table with two young de Medici boys who would become Popes of the Roman Catholic Church. His exposure to the lifestyle and connections of the de Medicis woud help shape his artistic life. Michaelangelo experienced the other end of Florentine life as well. He spent time at San Spirito doing anatomy studies of homeless penitents. It was an unusual opportunity for a teenager. Michelangelo learned the details of the human body that he would later capture in marble. It's interesting to note that I began my career as a psychologist working with heroin addicts. We shared the experience of working with people considered social outcasts by many of our peers. Undoutably, it influenced our world view and spirituality.

Romanesque Church, Carrara, Italy

I visited San Miniato al Monte during one of my trips to Florence. The Romanesque church sits at the top of the foothills across the Arno River hence the name "on the mountain". The view of Florence from the Piazzale Michelangelo is breathtaking. You can almost touch Il Duomo and the Ponte Vecchio. Michelangelo worked as a military achitect for the City of Florence and once suggested that they put mattresses around the bell tower to prevent any damage from a seige. It must have worked. The bell tower can still be seen behind the church. I made the slow, steep climb up "al monte" to study the delicate fescoes from the 11th Century as well as masterpieces from the Renaissance.

I took my time and stopped often during my ascent to San Miniato. A mountain of marble stairs beconed to me. I was drenched with sweat by the time I reached the door of the church. The cool temperature inside was a welcome relief and I was grateful to rest in this naturally air conditioned space.

Just as I sat down to catch my breath, the monks in residence at San Miniato began to sing noon prayers. Gregorian chant filled this beautiful Romanesque church. A Byzantine mosaic of the Pancreator blessed the small congregation as the monks sang. The concert lasted only 15 minutes. How lucky I was to be there! I didn't plan my visit to be able to hear the monks chant. It must have been a coincidence. It reminded me of my experience in Carrara where I was lucky enough to have a private organ concert in the church where Michelangelo worshiped. Luck? Coincidence? Or was I being moved, guided, to be in the right place at the right time to receive these special blessings? Special blessings? I wasn't even thinking in those terms yet. This sort of thing was to happen many, many times on my spiritual journey.

San Miniato al Monte, Florence, Italy

7

STANDING ON THE OUTSIDE

I took a lot of things for granted. I've always had the opportunity to earn extra money as a psychological consultant. In addition to working as a therapist and professor, I was asked do in-service training presentations and after dinner speeches. I would be called as an expert witness in a trial or to testify before a contract mediation panel. This kind of work was not predictable, not something to base a mortgage payment on, but was a nice source of "found money". Those opportunities always seemed to come when I had a need for extra cash. My car would need repairs or something would break around the house. It got to be such a regular pattern that when a new consulting job came along, I always wondered what was going to breakdown next. I was never in a bind. Financial stuff just worked out. I thought that was the way the world worked. I didn't think it was anything unusual.

A similar pattern developed in my work as a professor at the University of Detroit Mercy. I taught in the Psychology Department for 26 years and taught a variety of courses. From time to time, I would update my lectures or take on an entirely new course. Just like clockwork, the next catalogue from a textbook publisher would have exactly the book I needed or the American Psychologist would have a review of the literature I planned to cover. I never spoke with my colleagues about this phenomenon. I just thought it was par for the course.

I became a fine arts photographer when I retired from my career as a psychologist. The same kinds of coincidences occurred in my new career. I was always getting to a place where the light was perfect to shoot an award-winning photograph. I thought I was very lucky.

When I look back at my financial good luck, ease of accessing information for my classes, or ability to get to the right place at the right time for great photos, it seemed there were just too many coincidences, albeit happy coincidences. In those three important areas of my life, it looked as if someone was watching over me. I was thick headed and oblivious to the movement of the Holy Spirit in my life. I wasn't just lucky. I was blest.

I love Gothic cathedrals. Cathedrals housed the local bishop and were the most imposing structures in a medieval town. The Roman Catholic Church filled the void created by the collapse of the Roman Empire. The bishop assumed the role of the representative of the emperor and gave structure and order to daily life. Rather than represent the emperor, the bishop represented the pope and implemented the laws and policies of the Church in Rome. The Church provided a centralized government with a common set of laws for what was once the Roman Empire. Cathedrals represented government and religion, which were sometimes hard to distinguish. The cathedral was a symbol of wealth and economic success. Wealthy citizens and royalty would demonstrate their status by the magnitude of their contributions to the cathedrals.

I think most of us share the same awe as we walk into those soaring spaces with a forest of columns and glorious stained-glass windows. My spiritual journey took a long time, decades in fact. It certainly was not as well organized as my tours around the world. My spiritual journey might make more sense if I explain it as a walk through a church. I spent hundreds of hours walking through dozens of churches around the world. I absorbed a tremendous amount of knowledge and had incredible experiences. At the beginning of this journey, I would have described many of those experiences as bizarre, strange, and weird. I've come to value them as blessings and maybe even mystical experiences.

My spiritual journey picked up speed as I studied art in the most beautiful cathedrals in the world. Come with me to the front door of a cathedral. We will walk around the outside and then enter through the main portal. We'll make our way to the altar and admire the architecture and art along the way. It's a trek that millions of tourists make every year. Let's go together as pilgrims.

Basic Floor Plan of a Gothic Cathedral *

1 Facade
2 Facade Towers
3 Aisles
4 Nave
5 Portals

6 Transepts
7 Crossing Tower
8 Choir (apse)
9 Radiating Chapels
10 Ambulatory

Prepared by James R. Panyard. Used with permission.

Basic Floor Plan of a Gothic Cathedral, James R. Panyard

Most cathedrals face a large square. The squares in front of cathedrals are vibrant and full of life. They were the heart of the community. Squares were surrounded by businesses and markets were held there on a regular basis. Political rallies and competitions were conducted there as well. They were frequently lined with cafes and hosted impromptu musical performances. The square was the center of social life. It was the place to see and be seen. It's much the same today.

St. Peter's Square sits in front of St. Peter's Basilica in Vatican City. It has been the center of the Catholic Church since St. Peter preached there after the death and resurrection of Christ. His bones rest in a crypt beneath the soaring dome. Vatican City became an independent country in the middle of Rome in 1929. The faithful gather in the square to hear messages from the pope or word of the election of a new pope. Masses are said outside the basilica on special occasions to allow the maximum number of Catholics to participate in the liturgy. Of course, Tom Hanks appeared there many times in the Da Vinci Code movies. St. Peter's Square is one of the most recognizable places in the world.

I had a few hours to kill one day while I waited for my cousin to arrive in Rome. I wandered over to St. Peter's Square to enjoy the sunshine and watch the people. What could be better? I made my way through the monumental columns that surround the square and found more people than I had ever seen before. The square was packed. People were in groups wearing the same habits or sporting the same colors. Something very special was about to happen. I made my way to the center of the square near the obelisk and saw huge banners hanging from the front of the basilica. As soon as I found my place, Pope Benedict XVI mounted the altar in front of the cathedral. Gigantic flat screen televisions any sports venue would be proud to own were mounted at regular intervals around the square. I could barely see what was happening at the altar, but became part of the event thanks to the big screen TV's. Five men and women were about to become recognized as saints of the Catholic Church.

Canonization is a very lengthy process. It takes decades and sometimes hundreds of years for an individual's case to proceed through the steps required to become a saint. Saints are people who have led exemplary lives, have done incredible works, and have demonstrated extraordinary faith. Miracles attributed to their intersession are rigorously investigated before they can be elevated to sainthood. Catholics do not worship saints.

These men and women are venerated, held up as role models to the faithful. They are worthy examples of how to live a Christian life.

I could hardly believe my good fortune. I walked over to St. Peter's Square to kill some time and now I was going to participate in a papal Mass, a Canonization Mass. I hadn't planned to attend this great event. I didn't even know it was going to occur let alone at what time. It's an event many Catholics only dream about and there I was. Luck? Coincidence? It was happening again. Once more I was led to the right place at the right time to participate in an extraordinary event. I didn't even have an inkling that it might be the Holy Spirit working in my life. I was simply thrilled and excited to have wandered over to St. Peter's Square in time for such a wonderful occasion.

Cathedrals were built in different time periods, by different architects under the supervision of different bishops. It's not surpising that they are such unique structures. However, they are similar in their basic floor plan. The front of the cathedral is called the façade. It is the face that greets the pilgrim. It was designed to look grand and to humble the faithful before God and the Church.

Notre Dame de Paris is iconic. It sits in the heart of Paris on the Ile de France on the Seine River and calls to visitors from all over the world. This visitor was traveling solo and planned to spend an entire day in that section of Paris. I left my hotel early and arrived before 9:30AM. A temporary market celebrating French bread, La Fete du Pain, sprang up on the square in front of the cathedral. It was much more crowded than I had remembered. I entered and found banners proclaiming the celebration not only of bread, but of Acension Thursday, the day Christ ascended into heavan. It was a holy day of obligation and Catholics are required to attend Mass. It was a feast day I never kept holy. There were many excuses. I worked too late. The dogs needed to be let out. This Ascension Thursday would be different. I arrived as they were setting up for 10:00AM Mass, the high Mass for the holy day.

Notre Dame de Paris

The church was even more crowded than the square. Worshipers were separated from the tourists in the area in front of the altar. I joined the worshipers. At 10:00 AM sharp, the procession to the altar began with all the pomp the Catholic Church can muster. Priests, altar servers, and probably the Bishop of Paris walked down the far right aisle to the center of the church and then proceeded up the central aisle to the altar. A magnificent choir provided the music. They were so good they would have been at home performing with the New York Metropolitan Opera. I had never heard such beautiful renditions of familiar hymns. The cantors, the soloist who led the faithful in song, could have been stars in opera houses around the world. The smell of incense filled the cathedral. I hadn't planned on attending Mass that day. I didn't even know it was a holy day. What a coincidence. I found myself in Notre Dame de Paris at the right time to experience an incredible celebration. I was thrilled. I couldn't help but think about my mini concerts in Cararra and Florence and now high Mass at Notre Dame de Paris. They weren't as grand as the papal Canonization Mass in St. Peter's Square, but all were unexpected. Four extrodinary experiences in churches in a row. Coincidence?

The façades of Gothic cathedrals are very similar. Façade towers rise and give the impression that something very special is inside. Cathedrals took decades, sometimes over a hundred years to complete. The style in architecture or the technology might change during that time and the towers might be built very differently as in the case of Notre Dame de Chartres. Some were decorative and some housed bells. Think about the famous movie *The Hunchback of Notre Dame*. A rose window, named for its shape, lies beneath the towers and in the middle of the façade. The view from the outside is nice but not remarkable. The inside of the rose window is decorated in stained glass and is stunning. More about rose windows when we go inside the cathedral.

Cathedrals were picture books of the Catholic faith. Very few people could read in Medieval Europe and few could afford to have a Bible copied. The churches, inside and out, told the story of the faith. Gothic cathedrals had sculptural programs on the façade. The freize beneath the rose window of Notre Dame de Paris represented the kings of Israel in the Old Testament. Unfortunately, the French revolutionaries thought they were the kings of France and destroyed them after 1789 along with much of the façade. The kings were decapitated like Marie Antoinette. Their bodies and heads were found years later, but never properly reunited.

Notre Dame de Chartres

Façade Statuary, Cathedral of Cologne, Germany

The statues were often from familiar Biblical stories, the lives or saints, or represented the donors to the cathedral. I would like to be able to say exactly who these people are. The only one I recognize from the Cathedral in Cologne is Eve. The sculptural program on the façade and at the entrance could be used as a Catechism to teach the faithful. Medieval members of the congregation would understand the symbolism and could "read" the Bible as they walked around and through the cathedral.

The main entrances, or portals, to the cathedral were on the façade. The huge doors of each portal were separated by a doorjamb and, of course, it had a jamb statue. The doors were topped with tympanums. The tympanums were half circles or ovals that told an important story. The central door on the façade was the largest and its tympanum contained the story of the last judgment. Christ would be separating the saved from the damned. Devils would be dragging the damned to hell. The emotions on the faces of the people, as well as the devils, were portrayed vividly. The sculpture left no doubt in the minds of those walking through the door what might await them in the after-life. The smaller door to the left of the central portal frequently told stories of the life of the Virgin Mary, the Blessed Mother of Jesus. The story might be of her life or of her assumption to heaven and crowning as the Queen of Heaven.

The door to the right of the central portal usually told stories about Jesus. The tympanum of the church of St. Trophime in Arles, France shows Jesus and the four evangelists. The writers of the Gospels, Matthew, Mark, Luke and John, are represented by their symbols. Matthew is represented by an angel, Mark by a lion, Luke by an ox and John by an eagle. The tympanums are surrounded or framed, by sculptural programs called archivolts. The archivolts seem more personal. The archivolts told the stories of the people who built the cathedrals. The frames are formed by row after row of human figures. They might be angels, saints, craftsmen or townspeople. Local clergy, patrons who funded the project and even the oxen who lifted the huge stone blocks were often included. The sculptors seemed to have had more freedom in the archivolts. They didn't need to follow scripture as they would for the stories of the Last Judgment, Christ or the Blessed Mother. Freedom gave the sculptors the opportunity to insert at bit of humor in the program as well as give themselves credit for a remarkable feat.

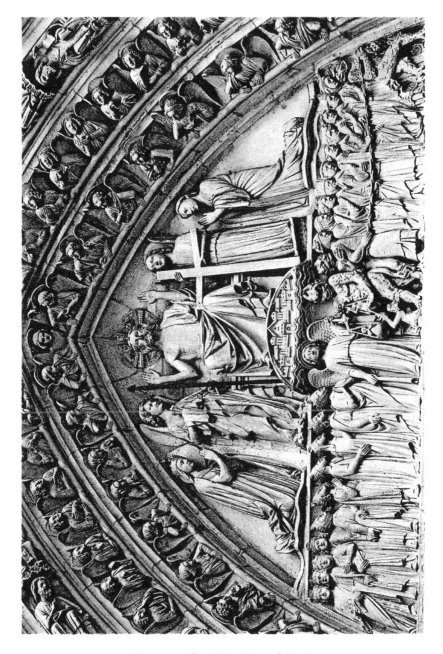

Tympanum from Notre Dame de Paris

Tympanum of St. Trophime in Arles, France

St. Trophime is a small Gothic church in Arles. It is a local parish church rather than a grand cathedral and located a short walk from the psychiatric hospital that once housed Vincent Van Gogh. It is dear to me because I had another of those special moments there. The longer I studied Gothic cathedrals and the more time I spent in the presence of the Blessed Sacrament, the more time I spent in prayer. I might just bless myself with Holy Water when I entered, say a rosary or occasionally find myself at Mass. My travel companion injured her knee at the beginning of our trip through France so she bowed out of the afternoon excursion in Arles. I was on my own, which is when those moments usually happened. I wandered back to St. Trophime intending to take a few more pictures of the Gothic arches and the gorgeous tapestries. My mother always carried a rosary in her purse and I picked up the habit from her. I took this time to sit by myself and prayed the rosary.

I was lost in prayer. I wasn't aware of what was going on around me. I don't know how long I was in that state. When I got up to leave, I found that I was the only person left in the church, except for the custodian. He stood at the back of the church and just smiled as I left. I learned later from my travel companions that he had shooed people out of the church. There was a wedding scheduled for that evening and he wanted to get the church ready without tourists in the way. But he left me to my prayer. He was probably dumbfounded to see an American tourist actually praying. Maybe he recognized that I was in a contemplative state. It was my first experience with the loss of self during contemplation. I floated back to my cruise ship. I experienced an incredible sense of wellbeing that I still feel when I recall the incident. It was such a wonderful experience, maybe my first mystical experience.

Most Gothic cathedrals are built in the form of a Roman cross. The aisle that forms the arms of the cross is called the transept. There are usually portals at the ends of the transepts. They have the same form as the portals on the façade with doors topped with tympanums and archivolts. However, the sculptural program is different. The portals on the north side typically tell stories from the Old Testament, a time of darkness before the coming of the Messiah. The sculptural program on the portals on the south side tell stories from the New Testament, a time of light with the coming of Christ.

Let's take a walk around the outside of the cathedral before we enter. The sides of Gothic cathedrals are full of very tall windows. When we go inside, we will find that they are gloriously colored stained glass. Glass is very fragile and could not withstand the weight of the stone roofs of Romanesque cathedrals. Two architectural developments made this change possible. The first was the development of pointed rather than rounded arches. They formed the interior supports and can be appreciated better once we enter the cathedral. They were able to hold more weight so the builders could reach greater heights. The second development was the buttress, an external support system that held the walls in place and allowed them to accept more force without collapsing. The force traveled down the buttresses to the ground taking the weight off the walls. This allowed the architects to design ever-taller cathedrals. It's interesting to think of the buttresses as the Church holding up the faith and the faithful.

The flying buttresses of Notre Dame de Paris are probably the most famous and most photographed. They extend far from the cathedral and are able to withstand even more force. They are placed around the apse or choir. It is where the clergy would sit and sing the Mass apart from the congregation. Gothic cathedrals were able to soar because they utilized the pointed arch and external buttresses, remarkable innovations in architecture.

You are bound to notice some very interesting sculptures as you walk around the outside of a Gothic cathedral. Gargoyles are horrible creatures that protrude from the walls and seem to leer at people passing by. They were designed in part to make people afraid to remain outside the church. They served a useful function as well. They were decorative ends of down spouts. Water needed to be removed from the roof and moved away from the walls. Water would weaken the foundation if it drained directly down the walls of the cathedral. Gargoyle sounds like gargle. We might get our word gargle from the sound of gargoyles doing their work. The creatures had a spiritual and functional purpose in addition to their artistic value.

I stood outside the Church for a long, long time. It was very difficult to go back after almost 15 years. I had been living in sin for most of that time. Would a priest even forgive all of my sins? I was married to a man who was not Catholic and at times seemed anti-Catholic. How would returning to Church affect my marriage? All kinds of questions and doubts kept me from returning. I started back to Church simply enough by going to Mass. The more I attended Mass, the more I felt the need to participate fully. So, I gathered my courage and made an appointment with my local pastor and took a giant step into the Church. I never realized that when I walked through the front door of so many cathedrals to study art, I was really coming back to Church.

Buttresses of Notre Dame de Paris

Gargoyles, Cathedral of Cologne, Germany

8

ENTERING THE HOUSE OF THE LORD

THE front door of the church opens to a narthex or vestibule that leads to the worship space. It represents a passage from the outside world to the house of God. It is the business end of the church. It holds hymnals, schedules of services, and a few paintings or statues to remind you that you have entered a church. Some narthexes are large enough to serve as gathering spaces for meetings and other church events. The narthex prepares you to enter a holy place. Modern churches may have a baptismal font in the narthex. It may be large enough for immersion and both children and adults can experience the initiation rite as it was first practiced. A separate building, the baptistery, was used during the Middle Ages and Renaissance. Members of the congregation would need to be baptized before they could enter the church and participate in Mass. Anyone may enter a cathedral or church today if they do so with reverence.

A second set of doors open to the nave, the central aisle of the church. It is the route worshipers take to their seats and the priest processes to the altar. Holy water fonts are placed at each door. They might be attached to the wall or free standing. They are filled with water blessed by a priest. Worshipers dip their fingers in the water and use it to make the sign of the cross. "In the name of the Father and the Son and the Holy Spirit" is the simple prayer said as one touches his forehead, heart, left shoulder and right shoulder. It is a sign and prayer repeated many times during the Mass. There are two additional aisles, one on each side of the nave. The nave and the aisles extend to the transept and the altar.

Nave of Sweetest Heart of Mary, a Neo-Gothic Church in Detroit, MI

The worshiper in a Gothic cathedral is assailed by the immensity of the space. It soars above you held up by colossal pillars and arches. I am fascinated, mesmerized by the arches. I love the regularity of their placement. It is awesome and calming at the same time. The arches remind me of arms sheltering the congregation. Some people see them as the hull of a large ship, maybe Noah's Ark, suspended above the congregation. I never tire of photographing them. Flecks of polychrome paint have been found in some cathedrals. It might be that they were painted, and probably gloriously, when they were completed. Today we see giant stone pillars carved with the simplest of tools. We are amazed how a people without modern equipment could have built such imposing structures. The backbreaking work was done with the use of oxen and a system of pulleys. You can find sculptures of oxen in some cathedrals. They are not always symbols of the evangelist St. Luke, but a tribute to the animals that lifted those pillars and arches into place.

The arches of the Early Gothic period were simple and utilitarian. Their purpose was to hold up the heavy roofs. They were beautiful and added to the majesty of the cathedral. They weren't the focal points they were to become later. Over time, the arches became more complex. More and more ribs were added for decorative purposes only. The amount and complexity increased until by the Baroque Period the arches were a distraction. Appropriately, the style was called Flamboyant Gothic. Later churches seemed to be vanity exercises for those who funded them. I would find myself trying to see and understand every detail rather than appreciate the holy space. I felt overwhelmed by the complexity rather than in the presence of God.

The interior of a Gothic cathedral has three levels. The aisles form the ground level. Originally it was empty and the congregation stood during the Mass. Today the space is filled with pews, wooden benches so the faithful may sit. The second level is the triforium. It looks like a gallery, but in most cases is not accessible. It helps to give height to the cathedral. By the Late Gothic period it was filled with windows. The third level is the clerestory where the fabulous stained-glass windows are installed. As architectural techniques improved, the thrust from the stone ceiling was transferred away from the walls. This allowed the delicate windows to be made ever taller.

Frauenkirche, Nuremburg, Germany

Westminster Abby, London, England

The stained-glass windows in Sainte-Chapelle in Paris take up more wall space than in any other structure. The chapel is just a few blocks from Nortre Dame de Paris. It was built to house a holy relic, the Crown of Thorns brought back by King Louis IX from the Holy Land. He went on to become St. Louis. The Crown of Thorns is kept at Notre Dame and brought out for special occasions.

The light from the stained-glass windows floods the interior of all cathedrals. The pattern changes as the sun makes its way across the sky. I spent an entire day at Notre Dame de Chartres so I could experience this first hand. Chartres is easy for a pilgrim to reach, just a short train ride from Paris. I went alone as a pilgrim and did not have to listen to a tour guide hurrying me along. I could bask in that glorious light as long as I wanted. The windows were removed during World War II to prevent damage or destruction during episodes of bombing. I can hardly imagine how difficult they were to remove and even more difficult to reassemble.

The stained-glass windows of Chartres are a picture book of the Catholic faith. It would take a lifetime to catalogue all the windows in Chartres and to explain the stories. If you did, you would have a visual catechism of the Catholic Church. The windows tell the stories of the Old Testament and the life of Christ. How to lead a Christian life, morality and redemption are presented. Saints are there as role models as well as part of our history. The people who contributed to the building fund as well as those who actually built the cathedral have honored places in the stained glass as well. One day would never be enough to appreciate the beauty and meaning of the stained-glass windows in Notre Dame de Chartres. I was blest to have an entire day so I could appreciate the changes in the stained glass as the sun moved across the sky and the cathedral. The experience was overwhelming. I took time to pray in that beautiful cathedral surrounded by the glowing stories of my faith.

One can spend so much time looking up at the arches and stained-glass windows in a cathedral that the floors get overlooked. The floors tell a story, too. The Medici Chapel in Florence, Italy is a marble wonder dedicated to the family most responsible for the Italian Renaissance. It is a mausoleum for those princes of commerce and supporters of artists of all kinds. The men are interred in the walls of the chapel. The women rest beneath the marble floor, a sad commentary on the role of women at that time. Their names and the dates of their time on earth mark their graves. Sometimes their likeness or attribute is carved on the marble slab. Most of those graves below the floor have not been protected and show the wear of the millions of feet that have trod on them. Some have completely lost their identifying information to the hordes of tourists who come every year. It's sad. They have been literally rubbed away from history.

The most famous cathedral floor is at Notre Dame de Chartres. A beautiful labyrinth is inlaid in the floor in the nave. Labyrinths have been around since antiquity and are found in many cultures. They represent a symbolic journey and can be walked as a substitute for the actual journey. They became popular in Medieval cathedrals as a substitute for a pilgrimage to the Holy Land. I can only imagine how difficult it would be to make a pilgrimage to Jerusalem in those days. Walking, riding a horse or in a horse drawn carriage would make it arduous. It would be difficult to find food and shelter. Monasteries were being established all over Europe at that time and functioned as the first motels. I stay at one run by the Trinitarian Fathers in Rome. They've been in business for over a thousand years and are very good at making pilgrims feel safe and welcome. A pilgrimage to the Holy Land was very dangerous. You would travel overland to the Mediterranean Sea, where you were likely to encounter pirates and unpredictable weather. If you survived the trip to a seaport and the sea crossing, you'd encounter hostilities between the Christians and Moslems. In addition, the journey would be very expensive and available only to the wealthy. No wonder labyrinths became so popular.

I planned my trip to Chartres for a Friday when I knew the chairs would be pushed back from the nave and pilgrims would be allowed to walk the famous labyrinth. I walked a canvass version in the activities center of my home church. This spiritual exercise was calming and enlightening so I made a point of visiting the real one. Many pilgrims pray the rosary, petition the Lord for favors or offer the journey as a thanksgiving for favors they have received. Most people stay on their feet, but some make the journey on their knees.

Walking the labyrinth at Notre Dame de Chartres turned out not to be a spiritual experience. The floor was very crowded and I had to pay attention to the traffic rather than the Lord. Some people moved at a snail's pace and it was difficult to get around the penitents on their knees. A group of Japanese tourists marched across the labyrinth oblivious to the fact that this was a spiritual exercise deserving respect. I had looked forward to this experience for a long time and it just wasn't working for me. I left feeling frustrated.

Notre Dame de Chartres, France

Labyrinth, Notre Dame de Chartres

I went outside and found a garden labyrinth behind the cathedral. Wonder of wonders, it was empty. I hurried down the stone stairs, hoping to complete this spiritual exercise before other tourists found it. It was much smaller and much simpler than the one inside. Most importantly, it would be mine alone. I entered the labyrinth prayerfully and headed to the first turn. It was like a maze in that you had the choice of which direction to turn. One direction would take you to the end of the journey and the other to a dead end. I paused and heard voices from above yelling, "droite" or "gauche". A group of college students were giving me directions. When I came to a choice point, they would tell me to go right or left, in French, of course. They applauded when I reached the end. I gave them my best diva bow. It was an entertaining experience, not the spiritual one I had sought. I've learned along the way that spiritual experiences are gifts from God and He gives them as He wants not as I would hope.

You will find confessionals as you walk down the side aisles of a cathedral. There are usually several on each side of the church. Some stand out from the wall and have the appearance of a closet or storage space. They have three small doorways just large enough for one person to enter. The center space is a bit larger and meant for the priest. He sits there to listen to the sins of the penitents who kneel on either side to confess their sins and receive absolution. A thick screen separates the priest from the penitent so the confession is not made face to face. There are panels of some sort between the priest and the screen so he can close one side after hearing a confession and then open the panel to the other confessional to listen to another sinner. The doors to the confessionals, heavy curtains and panels function to sound proof the space so no one other than the priest can hear one's confession.

The Sacrament of Penance or Reconciliation involves the forgiveness of sins as well as reconciliation with the Church. It has a long history in the Catholic Church. Jesus said to Simon Peter, after the Resurrection, "I will give you the keys of the kingdom of heaven, and whatever you bind on earth shall be bound in heaven, and whatever you loose on earth shall be loosed in heaven." John 20:23. Other translations put it more simply, "Whose sins you forgive are forgiven them, and whose sins you retain are retained." The power given by Jesus to Peter has been passed down to priests through apostolic succession. All priests are ordained by a bishop who had been ordained by another bishop. The Sacrament of Ordination continues an unbroken line all the way back to St. Peter. The Sacrament of

Reconciliation heals the damage done to our relationship with God as well as our relationships with others and our community.

When a person confesses his sins to a priest, he is acknowledging that he has done something very wrong and is willing to take responsibility for making amends. The priest gives absolution, and then gives a penance to the penitent. Penance is a way of making amends for one's transgressions. The most common forms are prayer, sacrifice and alms giving. Those are the same things that all Catholics are asked to do during penitential periods in the liturgical year like Lent and Advent.

We don't take sin very seriously anymore but it is very serious business. It impacts the community far beyond the individual sinner. In the Old Testament, entire communities were punished. Only Noah and his passengers on the ark survived the flood that destroyed the rest of humanity. Many people perished in the earthquake that opened the ground near the golden calf worshiped by the Israelites while Moses received the Ten Commandments on Mt. Sinai. The entire nation of Israel did penance for their lack of trust in God during the 40 years they wandered in the desert before entering the Promised Land. Sin compromises an individual's ability to function and endangers an entire community.

I worked as a psychologist for 43 years and heard many confessions from substance abusers and police officers. I certainly couldn't forgive sins, but helped people to forgive themselves. I witnessed firsthand the powerful effects of clients sharing their burdens. Telling someone else those deep, dark secrets reduces the guilt people carry around for years, sometimes decades. It feels good. It is a relief. Psychologists call this abreaction or catharsis. Believe me, people give themselves far worse penances than a priest ever would. So why did it take me so long to go to Confession?

I was embarrassed and afraid to go to confession. I was supposed to know better. After all, I was a psychologist. I was supposed to have everything under control. At least I was supposed to be able to control my base impulses. I was a flawed human being and finally able to admit that I had made mistakes, serious mistakes. I was afraid that the priest might not forgive me or give me a horrendous penance I wouldn't be able to complete. I was afraid that my parish priest might not like me after hearing my sins. I didn't realize that the priest was only functioning as a good shepherd trying to get one more lost sheep back into the fold.

I had been away from Church for 15 years and had a lot to confess. This would take some time. I arranged for an individual appointment with my local priest rather than a quick visit to a confessional. It was my first confession in many years and my very first face-to-face confession. Face-to-face confessions were introduced after Vatican II in the 1960's. I would be sitting across from the priest just like my clients sat across from me. I would not have the anonymity of a confessional. The priest was very kind and non-judgmental. He didn't order me to wear sack- cloth and ashes or abstain from meat for three years or live with my husband as brother and sister. He absolved me of my sins and must have given me an easy penance because I don't remember what it was. Two weeks later the priest showed up in my graduate psychology class at the University of Detroit Mercy. I was mortified! My confessor was now my student. God does have a sense of humor.

Even though I had done everything prescribed for a good confession, I still didn't feel completely absolved. I confessed the same old sins many times even in the Vatican. I felt cleaner, but not fully healed. I'm blest to live in a retirement community that has a chapel for community worship. One of the sacristies is a walk-in-tabernacle that is used for individual prayer, my own private adoration chapel. I was meditating on the sculpture of Christ at the pillar, the place where He was scourged after being condemned to death by Pilate. It portrays the pain and sorrow Christ felt at the beginning of his Passion. His agony, His suffering was intense. I was gifted with a successive locution, my second. A successive locution is a voice in your head that follows from a meditative state. It's not hearing voices in the room, but in your head as a result of prayer. I heard Jesus say, "Chris, look what I did to redeem you. You have been forgiven." WOW! I felt abreaction, catharsis, and finally forgiveness. My soul was closer to being healed. If that had happened to me a few years earlier, I would have feared it a sign of psychosis. Now I recognized it as a great blessing.

The Stations of the Cross are usually above the confessionals but below the stained-glass windows. They represent the path Jesus walked on his way to Calvary. The Stations of the Cross consist of 14 numbered pictures that portray the events from the time He was condemned to death until He was laid in the tomb after His crucifixion. It is an imitation of the Via Dolorosa in Jerusalem said to be the actual path Christ walked. Mel Gibson's 2004 movie *The Passion of the Christ* follows the traditional Stations of the Cross. The stations can be constructed of any material and can be found in gardens as well as churches.

Detail of the Passion Façade of the Sagrada Familia, Barcelona, Spain

The Stations of the Cross, sometimes called the Way of the Cross, is a devotional exercise. The faithful walk from station to station and say prayers before each station. It is a spiritual pilgrimage, much like a labyrinth, that allows the pilgrim to share in Christ's passion. Stations of the Cross are found in a variety of Christian churches including Anglican, Lutheran, Methodist and Roman Catholic. It's most likely to be prayed during Lent.

St. Francis of Assisi founded the Custody of the Holy Land in 1217 to protect holy places in what is now Israel. Pope Clement VI gave the Franciscans that responsibility officially in 1342 and they continue in that role today. I was blest to go to the Holy Land with Terra Sancta Pilgrimages, a Franciscan organization in 2015. We were able to see the Holy Land as only a Franciscan could arrange. Our pilgrimage included the opportunity to pray the Stations of the Cross on the Via Dolorosa in Jerusalem, the actual path that Jesus took on Good Friday.

Our wake-up call was at 4:15 AM and we were on our way to Old Jerusalem by 5:00AM. It was an ungodly hour but it paid off. We were able to avoid the heat and the crowds that would clog the streets later in the day. We were alone. The streets were dark and quiet. I wanted this to be a prayerful experience rather than a photo shoot, so I left my camera in its case.

Three pilgrims at a time took turns carrying a life-sized cross as we walked the Via Dolorosa. Our cross was heavy and difficult to carry over the uneven paving stones. The streets were very dirty and filled with the stink of yesterday's trash. I could only imagine what it would have been like filled with unwashed people yelling and jeering at us. Pack animals, vermin and dogs would have added to the stench. It was a struggle for three able bodied people to lug our cross through the narrow streets of Old Jerusalem. How agonizing it would have been for Jesus to carry His cross after having been beaten and scourged. Every breath and every step would have been tortuous. Our journey through Via Dolorosa was strenuous, but we were never in agony. We didn't look forward to a shameful death on the cross at the end. No wonder Jesus fell three times along the way. It was incredible that Jesus made it to Calvary alive. We stopped at all fourteen stations and said the traditional prayers. It was a deeply moving experience that engaged all of our senses, thoughts and feelings. Praying the Stations of the Cross on the Via Dolorosa brought us closer to the passion of Christ. I knew that I would pray the Stations of the Cross in a clean, safe church again. This beautiful prayer would never be the same after having carried a life-sized cross in the footsteps of Christ.

Continuing our journey down the aisles in a cathedral, you'll find many small chapels. Wealthy members of the parish funded them and they became status symbols. The greatest painters and sculptors of the day were hired to attest to the patron's worth. The Medici of Florence were wealthy enough to hire Michelangelo. These chapels hold some of the most famous works of art in the world. Many side chapels became mausoleums for high society families. The chapels had altars and priests were hired to say Mass daily for members of the family who had departed.

The cathedral in Palermo, Sicily is one of the most beautiful in Italy. It is immense, part crusader, part Gothic and absolutely gorgeous. Unfortunately, I was there on tour rather than a pilgrimage and only had 30 minutes to explore it. I crossed the nave and turned right at the first aisle. I was stopped in my tracks by a statue of St. Cristina VM. The VM stands for virgin martyr. Next to the statue was a chapel that purported to hold her remains. I was standing in front of the crypt that held the body of my namesake! How weird was that? I still had a long way to go before I considered such "coincidences" blessings, rather than weird or crazy experiences.

In the days before names like Megan and Taylor became popular, Catholic babies had to be baptized with the name of a saint of the Church. Your saintly namesake would be your spiritual godparent. *The Golden Legend* was written around 1260 by Jacobus de Voragine. It's a compendium of lives of the saints and it is where I encountered the first St. Cristina. She was born to a highly ranked family in the third century after Christ. Her father wanted to consecrate her to his gods. Unfortunately, she had become a Christian and consecrated herself to Christ. She endured horrendous tortures at the hands of her father including being beaten, flayed and thrown into the sea with a stone tied around her neck. She was cast into a burning furnace and surrounded by poisonous snakes. Her breasts and tongue were cut off. Finally, she was shot through with three arrows and breathed her last. St. Cristina never denied her new faith and was martyred about 287 AD. Her body was placed near Bolsena in southern Italy. Could these actually be her remains in the great cathedral of Palermo?

I found two other St. Christina's in *The Big Book of Women Saints*, St. Christina of Markyate (England, d. 1160) and Blessed Christina the Astonishing (Belgium, d. 1224). Both refused to marry and spent part of their lives as Benedictine nuns. Whew! That's an awful lot to live up to. I'm sure I will probably not follow in their footsteps but will continue my own journey.

Crypt of St. Cristina, Cathedral of Palermo, Italy

The side aisle in a cathedral begins to curve as you approach the altar. It becomes the ambulatory, a walkway that takes you around the altar and down the other side aisle.

Chapels radiate from the ambulatory. These are similar to the chapels that line the aisles in the main body of the cathedral. The ambulatory of St. Anne de Beaupre in Quebec City, Canada is my favorite. I know, who has a favorite ambulatory? The French built the first church on this site in 1658. The current and fifth basilica was built in 1923. It is neo-Romanesque and very modern. I was there with Prayer Pilgrimages as part of a tour of historic churches in Toronto, Montreal and Quebec City. We spent the night at a guesthouse on the grounds and had ample time to explore and pray.

I took my time moving down the aisle towards the altar, stopping often to take photographs of statues and stained glass. The ambulatory was roped off. A member of the staff met me near the altar. We chatted about the historic St. Anne's Church in Detroit built by the French in 1701. He asked if I was staying for Mass. Yes. Was I going to be part of the candlelight procession and veneration of St. Anne's relics? Yes. Would I carry a banner in the procession? How could I say "no"? He opened the roping and beckoned me up the stairs to the ambulatory. He closed the entrance and said, "Just make sure that this is closed when you leave."

It was heavenly. Chapels lined the ambulatory and every chapel was more beautiful than the previous one. Stories from the life of Christ were told in golden mosaics. Each one captured light and showered it on the visitor lucky enough to be there. The colors were bright and intense. I took photographs and then sat down to pray. I was in the ambulatory for 45 minutes, alone. No one came to join me. No fellow pilgrim or member of the staff disturbed my experience. It was wonderful and I was floating again. I could hardly contain my joy. I couldn't understand why I had been so lucky to enjoy solitude in this holy space. I learned much later that it wasn't luck. I've come to understand that my experience in St. Anne's ambulatory was a very private encounter with the Divine.

My prayer time in St. Anne's was similar to finishing my prayers in an empty church in Arles or entering St. Peter's Square with Pope Benedict XVI for a canonization Mass. They were gifts from the Holy Spirit. It is difficult to write these words because to a psychologist they really do sound crazy. There was no doubt that I was having incredible, beautiful, spiritual experiences in churches around the world. But why were they being given to me? I was just a senior citizen with a past, no one special. Were the experiences only for my personal joy? What was I to do with them? I simply wrote them down in my journal.

I was reluctant to share my experience with other members of the pilgrimage. Would they think I was making up a story, trying to look holy? Would there be a spiritual competition with pilgrims vying for the most spiritual experience? Would they think I might be going crazy, too? I closed the roping behind me and left the ambulatory for evening Mass and the procession. I walked down the nave of St. Anne's to find a seat.

Walking down the nave of a cathedral or any Catholic church is much like walking into the Tabernacle YHWH commanded Moses to build. It was to be the dwelling place of God. Approximately one third of the Book of Exodus in the Old Testament contains detailed directions for the construction of the Tabernacle, which attests to its importance to God. The first Tabernacle was to be a portable structure the Hebrews could carry with them in the desert. It became permanent as the Temple in Jerusalem.

The public would enter the temple through a courtyard similar to the narthex in a church. It is the beginning of movement towards God, but is not a holy place. Business and socializing can occur in both the courtyard and a narthex. A variety of sacrifices were performed on the altar in the Tabernacle. A laver, or ritual cleaning bowl was behind the altar. In a Catholic church, the sacrifice of the Mass is celebrated on an altar. The priest washes his hands before the consecration and the faithful bless themselves with Holy Water when then enter the church. Both are cleansing rituals.

A smaller area within the temple was reserved for the priests. It was separated from the public by a screen. Cathedrals were built with a separation between the public and the priests as well. The choir was an area at the intersection of the nave and the transept. It was reserved for the clergy and separated from the public by a rood screen, an ornate wooden structure. The rood screens came down with the Counter Reformation but the altar remained in the sanctuary and separated from the people by a communion rail. In the temple, this area contained a table for twelve loaves of bread representing the Twelve Tribes of Israel. It also contained a lampstand with seven branches that symbolized the tree of life and an incense altar. A heavy curtain separated this area from the Holy of Holies, the place where the ark rested. The ark contained the Ten Commandments and Aaron's rod. The Holy of Holies could only be approached by the High Priest and only at special times of the year.

Ambulatory, Basilica of St. Anne de Beaupre, Quebec City, Canada

In a Catholic church, the Tabernacle was on the main altar where Mass was celebrated. The priest faced the Tabernacle while he performed his priestly duties. After Vatican II the altar was moved towards the people and the priest faces them as he celebrates Mass now. The communion rail has been removed in most churches so there is no barrier between the priest and the people. The Tabernacle in a cathedral is located on the "old" main altar. In modern churches it might be behind the 'new" main altar or in a tabernacle chapel outside of the sanctuary. The Tabernacle in a Catholic church is very similar to the Holy of Holies in a temple. God says in Exodus 25:8, "Let them make me a sanctuary, that I may dwell in their midst." The Tabernacle in a Catholic church and the Holy of Holies in the temple are God's earthly dwelling places.

Elaborate altarpieces were constructed to house the Tabernacle. They could be sculptural, precious metals encrusted with jewels or paintings. They were required to be very heavy and locked to prevent anyone from taking and desecrating the consecrated hosts. Catholics and other Christians believe the Doctrine of Transubstantiation. The bread and wine offered on the altar becomes the very body and blood of Jesus during the consecration. The consecrated hosts don't merely represent or symbolize Jesus. The bread and wine are Jesus. A red lamp in the sanctuary near the altar lets the faithful know that consecrated hosts, Jesus, are in the Tabernacle.

The altar in a Catholic church is where the Mass is celebrated. It is no longer against the wall beneath the Tabernacle. It is presented as a table closer to the congregation so that the act of sharing a meal with other faithful and the Lord seems more real. The altar is usually made of stone but can be of any material. My father told the story of how during World War II the priest assigned to his unit said Mass on the hood of a jeep. It was more important to celebrate Mass in a reverential manner for men going into battle than to worry about the material used for the altar. Usually, authenticated relics of saints are placed in or under the altar to enhance its importance.

The altar in a Catholic church is covered with a white linen cloth. Paraments, decorative ecclesiastical hangings, might be found under the white cloth. Their color indicates the liturgical season of the year. For example, the paraments during Lent and Advent are purple to indicate that those are penitential times. The priest's vestments match the color of the paraments. A Bible open to the Gospels and two candles are placed on the altar cloth. During Mass, the candles are lit and the Bible remains on the altar until it's time for the priest to proclaim the Gospel.

Tabernacle, Cathedral of Rothenburg, Germany

I explored Catholic Churches for about ten years while I studied Michelangelo and Renaissance art. I never considered how being in the presence of the Blessed Sacrament would affect me. I just went about the business of studying art and history and taking photographs of everything. The change in me was imperceptible. All the time I thought I was studying art I was being drawn to the altar, drawn to the Lord. At first, I would stop at the grave of someone I admired and say "thank you" to God for having blessed the world with his or her talents. My prayers increased, first a thank you, then an Our Father. Pretty soon I was saying the Rosary or attending Mass. It wasn't planned. I didn't see it coming but I was moving closer to Jesus all the same.

A crucifix is placed on or near the altar. Sometimes it rests in a stand and sometimes it is suspended from the ceiling. It must be visible to all attending Mass. A crucifix differs from a cross in that it has a representation of the body of Christ. It is a graphic reminder of the sacrifice Christ became to redeem our sins. The crucifix has played an important role in the history of the Church. St. Francis of Assisi was praying beneath one in his home church of San Damiano when he heard a voice say, "Fix my Church." Francis heard, "Fix my church" and set about repairing churches. Eventually, he got the message straight and began reforms to repair the Catholic Church not individual parish churches.

Candles play an important role in the decoration, liturgy and prayer of the Church. Originally, they were used as a source of light. Today they represent reverence and prayer. At least two lit candles are on the altar during Mass. Any number may be used as decoration on special occasions as long as they do not obscure what is happening on the altar. Many Christian denominations hold candlelight services for special occasions like Easter and Christmas. It's a wonderful sight to see the church lit by candles held by everyone in the congregation. The candles enhance the holiness of the space and the service that is about to begin.

Candles are found in the chapels that line the walls of a cathedral as well as at the front of a church. They are usually just outside of the sanctuary so they can be lit by the faithful. Some churches have a separate votive chapel filled with candles that can be offered with prayers. Lighting a candle is an act of supplication, a tangible sign of asking a favor of God. It may also be an act of gratitude for favors already granted. Catholics don't believe that their prayers ascend to God in the candle smoke. Lighting a candle is a sign of faith that our prayers will be lifted up to the Lord.

Crucifix, Cathedral of Wertheimer, Germany

St. Michael's Church was near my hotel in Volterra, Italy. The Roman-esque church was dark and quiet, just the way I like them. The different heights of the candles indicated that people had come in throughout the day to offer prayers. When I returned a few days later for Sunday Mass I found the church closed. A sign said to go to the Cathedral instead of this neighborhood church. I walked to the other end of Volterra and found quite a crowd gathering. I joined the faithful and discovered that an ordina-tion was about to occur. This would be my first and I looked forward to the ceremony. A young man would take vows of obedience, poverty and chastity and pledge his life to the service of the Lord. I squeezed into a pew and waited for the ceremony to begin. Two women joined me. They were artists and I met earlier in the day when I visited their studio. What a coincidence that the only two women I recognized in the crowd, and who recognized me, sat beside me at the ordination. Their English was as good as my Italian and they kept me on track throughout the ceremony. What a wonderful and unexpected experience. I recognized it as gift from the Holy Spirit and not just another crazy, strange, weird coincidence. I was starting to get the message.

St. Michael Church, Volterra, Italy

9

THE MASS

THE very front of the church, at the end of the nave, is the most holy part of a cathedral. The altar, the table of the Lord, is where Holy Mass is celebrated. The Mass is much more than a prayer service. It is the most important prayer offed by the Catholic Church. It is the re-enactment of the Last Supper when Christ shared bread and wine with his disciples as his body and blood. It is referred to as the Sacrifice of the Mass because the bread and wine become the body and blood of Christ, who was sacrificed to redeem us from sin. Catholics are obliged to attend Mass every Sunday and on Holy Days of Obligation. We are encouraged to attend often. Some people go every day and are called daily communicants because they receive the Holy Eucharist daily.

My first weird, crazy, strange experience related to churches occurred at Mass at Santa Maria Maggiore, a papal basilica in Rome. My friend Mary Hannah and I were on our own in Rome for the first time. I planned our adventure without the benefit of a travel agent or tour guide. Our first day in Rome was brutal. After an overnight flight, we pretended there was no such thing as jet lag. We spent the remainder of the day walking between Santa Maria Maggiore, Saint John Lateran, Saint Clement, and San Pietro in Vincoli. We walked much too far for two middle aged professors. We had planned to meet Mary's cousin the next morning after nine o'clock Mass. Not surprisingly, we over-slept and needed to change our plans. We went to 10:00 o'clock Mass and arrived in time to participate in the 50th Anniversary celebration of a cardinal's ordination. The procession down the nave to the altar included acolytes carrying incense and candles. The cardinal and about 20 of his closest friends dressed in their clerical splendor followed the acolytes. What sounded like a professional choir provided the music for the event. It was all the pomp and ceremony that the Catholic Church could muster. How lucky were we to have overslept! It was a wonderful experience and the first of many spiritual gifts I was to receive.

The Vatican, the ruling body of the Roman Catholic Church, determines the content of the Mass. A Mass said in St. Peter's Square, in a grotto chapel in the Holy Land or at neighborhood church are essentially the same. The format and the readings are shared worldwide. Before Vatican II, it was said in Latin. Latin may still be used, but most Masses are celebrated in the local language, the vernacular. A Catholic may participate in the Mass anywhere in the world and feel at home. The language and choice of hymns may differ, but the structure, order and meaning are the same everywhere. The similarities are comforting and allow all to participate in the supper of the Lord. The church, the mystical body of Christ, worships the Lord as one family. It's absolutely phenomenal that one billion Catholics celebrate the Mass using the same ritual. Given the extent of the Church, Mass is probably being said at every hour of the day.

The Mass has three parts: Introductory Rites, the Liturgy of the Word, and the Liturgy of the Eucharist. The Introductory Rites set the stage for what is to come. The altar servers, the lectors and the priest process down the nave, the center aisle, while the congregation sings a hymn. It's time to put down the church bulletin and rosary and focus your attention on the Mass. After greeting the congregation, the priest asks us to "acknowledge our sins, and so prepare ourselves to celebrate the sacred mysteries." We are asked to reflect on where we have erred. The entire congregation, including the priest, recites the Confiteor, an act of contrition. General absolution is given to cleanse us and prepare us to receive the Holy Eucharist. A general absolution is not the same as participating in the Sacrament of Reconciliation. It will not absolve one of mortal sins, those sins judged to be very grave. That takes a private confession with a priest. We praise God by reciting or singing the Gloria, except during the penitential seasons of Advent and Lent, and are ready to hear the Word of God.

Canonization Mass, St. Peter's Square, Rome

The ambo is a very ornate structure that rises before the altar. From where the congregation sits, it is on the left side of the cathedral. The priest mounts the stairs and reads the scripture passage for the day. He delivers the homily from there as well. The ambo is high enough so that the priest may be seen from almost any place in the cathedral. The ambo in a cathedral usually has a cupola or shell above the rostrum. This functions as a sounding board. In the days before high tech sound systems, it bounced the priest's voice to the people. The ambo worked well to project the priest's power and status as well as his voice.

Amos, a prophet from the Old Testament, said, "The time is surely coming, says the Lord God, when I will send a famine on the land; not a famine of bread, or a thirst for water, but of hearing the words of the Lord," Amos 8:11. We listen to the Word of God during the second part of the Mass, the Liturgy of the Word. Typically, the lector reads from the Old Testament, Psalms, and epistles. The priest reads from the Gospel and gives a homily based on the day's readings. The readings are selected by the Church to reflect the liturgical season of the year. It was surprising to me to learn that many Protestant denominations use the same order of readings used during a Catholic Mass. The Liturgy of the Word ends with a recitation of the Nicene Creed, which is a summary of Catholic teachings, and with prayer requests.

The third, and most important part of the Mass is the Liturgy of the Eucharist. That is the time of the Consecration, when the bread and wine are transformed into the Body and Blood of Christ. Only the priest can say these prayers. He has been ordained to continue the line from the first apostles and is able to repeat the miracle of the Last Supper. The priest prays, "Take this, all of you, and eat of it, for this is my body . . . Take this all of you, and drink from it, for this is the chalice of my blood." This is the holiest moment in the Mass.

Ambo, Notre Dame de Montreal, Canada

The moment of consecration became difficult for me in my home parish. I started to have all kinds of strange physical symptoms just at the time I was supposed to be most focused on the Lord. I would feel light-headed and fear that I was about to pass out. I would have coughing and sneezing fits. Hot flashes I hadn't had in 10 years would drench me in sweat. These sensations only occurred during the consecration. I didn't experience them at home, with friends or walking through a museum. It's difficult for people to stay focused on the Mass. I know that. Our minds wander and many things distract us. However, I thought my reaction was a bit extreme. It felt as if something was working to keep me from participating fully in the consecration. I also know that sounds a bit crazy. I couldn't imagine that any evil spirits would be that interested in my little soul but I couldn't think of any other reason for the strange experience.

Our pastor gave a presentation on angels once. He mentioned that we had a team working for us. I never thought about it in those terms. I had always prayed to the Blessed Mother and St. Jude, the patron of hopeless cases, when I was frightened. St. Michael the Archangel seemed like a good addition to my team. St. Michael the Archangel is revered for having driven Satan from heaven. Surely, he could send his assistants to drive my demons away during Mass. I started praying to him before Mass and, low and behold, those strange physical symptoms that had been keeping me from participating fully in the Mass disappeared. St. Michael was really on my team.

The Liturgy of the Eucharist is a banquet. We participate in the celebration Jesus Christ instituted at the Last Supper. The apostles who had been called to serve the Lord shared in his body and blood. Members of the congregation who are in communion with the Roman Catholic Church are invited to participate in the supper of Our Lord. Members of the church who have made their First Communion, have fasted for one hour, and are currently in the state of grace may receive the Holy Eucharist.

It would be wonderful if we were still "one, holy, catholic and apostolic Church," but we are very divided. There may be many people in the church who do not qualify to receive communion. They may not share the beliefs of the Roman Catholic Church or may not be properly prepared to receive the Holy Eucharist. Members of Orthodox Churches, the Assyrian Church of the East, and the Polish National Catholic Church may receive communion in a Roman Catholic Church. There are hundreds of Christian denominations, some very similar to the Roman Catholic and some sharing only the name Christian. Members of those denominations are not allowed to receive communion during Mass. They are encouraged to come to the altar with hands crossed over their chest to receive a blessing from the priest. It would be contrary to Canon Law for them to receive the Holy Eucharist. Of course, they may remain prayerfully in their seats.

Catholics didn't receive Holy Communion very often when the Gothic cathedrals were being built. It was common only during Easter and Christmas. The fasting requirements were much stricter and very few members of the congregation received communion each Sunday, let alone every day of the week. The clergy were the only ones who received communion frequently. Today, most members of the congregation receive communion at every Mass they attend. We stand before the priest or Eucharistic Minister, a layperson trained to give communion, and may receive it on the tongue or in our hands. We may receive it in both species, meaning both bread and wine. In some churches, people still kneel at a communion rail to receive communion. Communicants return to their seats and pray quietly while communion is distributed to the rest of the congregation.

The priest spends time purifying the vessels used in the ceremony and straightening the altar. The Concluding Rites begin when he has finished his housekeeping duties. Announcements are read and a final blessing is given. The priest says, "The Mass has ended. Go in peace, glorifying the Lord by your life," concluding the celebration. The priest and his assistants recess from the church to the sound of a closing hymn. The people follow the priest to the narthex. Now it's the time to socialize with other members of the congregation. Most people feel spiritually uplifted after Mass. They may have learned something useful during the Liturgy of the Word or have been inspired by the homily. Hopefully, they feel better able to tackle the day and the week before them.

The effects of the Mass are cumulative. You're not likely to be inspired or enlightened every time you go. It's important to attend regularly because it does change you. The changes are usually gradual, imperceptible. You'll find that you enjoy the celebration and actually miss it when you can't attend. You might find yourself becoming more involved in the life of the parish, attending a class on spiritual development or community building. You might be drawn to spiritual reading or become a member of a special ministry. All the while, God is drawing you into a closer, deeper relationship with Himself and the Church. That's how it worked for me.

Liturgy of the Eucharist, Solanus Casey Beatification Mass, Detroit, MI

10

GO IN PEACE, GLORIFYING
THE LORD BY YOUR LIFE

W ALKING through a Gothic cathedral is a powerful experience. It puts
me in a state of sensory overload. The sights, sounds and smells of
a distant era overwhelm me. I've studied cathedrals all over the world and
studied them as diligently as I had studied psychology. I spent ten years as a
full-time college student before I earned my Ph.D. in counseling. My spiri-
tual development took a long time, too. I never realized that spending so
much time in the house of God, in the presence of the Blessed Sacrament,
would have such a powerful effect on me. It was after ten years of studying
and photographing cathedrals that the Lord called me. There was no clap
of thunder or vision in the Sistine Chapel. I was gradually being nudged
towards the Lord. As I walked down the naves of too many cathedrals to
count, I was really walking towards the Lord.

I am like the laborers in the vineyard who were called late in the day.
According to Matthew 20, a landowner went out several times in one day
to get laborers for his field. He called the first laborers at dawn and the last
in late afternoon. He made an agreement with each to pay them a fair day's
wage. When it came time to settle with them, he paid the last first and gave
them a full day's wages. When it came time to pay those called first, he paid
them a full day's wages as well. Not surprisingly, they complained about
the unfairness of the landowner. The landowner held his ground and stated

that he was free to do what he wanted with his money. The landowner rewarded all the laborers equally for their work as he had promised.

The Lord started calling me long before I took the time to hear Him. I worked, and worked and worked and didn't listen. I didn't start to hear the Lord until I was in my 60's. I know that my work as a psychologist was a calling. I was blest to be able to touch people as a therapist and a professor. It was a professional and academic calling, surely nothing spiritual. The Lord called to me in a way I could understand, through my work as a researcher and writer.

I began writing my first book, *The Sistine Chapel, A Biblical Tour,* in 2007. I was on fire. I couldn't get enough of Michelangelo, Renaissance art or scripture. The first 49 publishers rejected it. The religious publishing houses said it had too much art in it and the art houses said it had too much religion. I wasn't disappointed or discouraged. I looked at each rejection as confirmation that I hadn't found the right publisher yet. I remained confident that one was out there. Finally in 2008, Paulist Press, the largest Catholic publishing house in the United States, agreed to publish it. It languished for five years before we secured the images from the Vatican and I held it in my hands.

Members of the staff at the University of Detroit Mercy were happier for me than my colleagues. Most professors were dismissive of my new work. After all, it was for the general public and not an academic audience. It was so outside of my field. It could have no gravitas. Luckily, or so the Lord planned, it was at the end of my academic career. I was already a Full Professor and would never need their approval again. I retired shortly after the book was published and embarked on a new career.

I couldn't stop writing. I produced A Renaissance Christmas, A Renaissance Easter and The End of Times in Renaissance Art. Those projects followed the format of my first book and brought together Renaissance art and the scripture they illustrated. I knew they weren't worthy of publication, and they became presentations at my church. I was writing and doing research on art and scripture and teaching about beauty and spirit much as I had about psychology. I looked back on these exercises as training for my new profession. The projects kept me in churches and museums all over the world. My home became filled with museum catalogues and heavy tomes about the great masters. My knowledge of Renaissance art and scripture increased dramatically and I continued to be exposed to the Blessed Sacrament. As Kevin Gould would say, "God was qualifying the called".

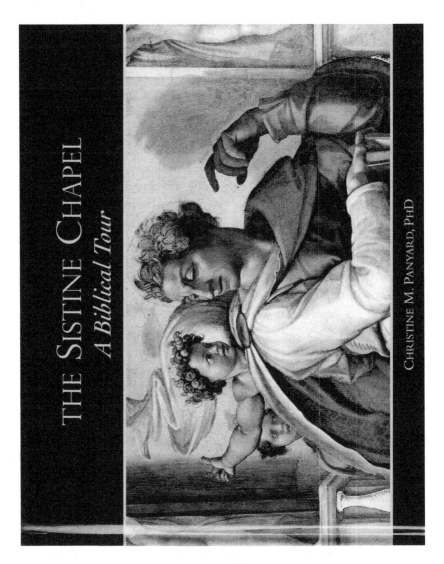

The Sistine Chapel
A Biblical Tour

Christine M. Panyard, PhD

My Book

Publishing someone else's images is very expensive so I started taking my own photographs. An old boyfriend, who happened to be a photographer, gave me a list of everything I needed for digital photography and I was off on a new endeavor. I always seemed to be in the right place at the right time to get great shots. I would get to a cathedral in time for a Papal Canonization Mass or an Ordination. Monks and organists would begin to perform as soon as I sat down in their churches. I would get to a location at exactly the right time to capture dramatic shadows. The effect would not have been there if I had arrived ten minutes earlier or later. It was uncanny. The coincidences were happening too often to be coincidences and I thought I might be going crazy. I learned later that I wasn't crazy. I was being deluged with blessings.

The Holy Spirit was getting me to the right place at the right time to produce beautiful art of my own. I started exhibiting my photographs in local shows in 2015 and always included a religious photo. Sometimes they were juried out of the show and no one saw them but the judge. More often, my work won awards. My work won four first place awards for photography in four consecutive shows of the Artists Society of Dearborn. Of course, I post my work on Facebook and write something about the significance of the work. My Facebook work follows the Church's liturgical year. I post pictures of the Madonna and Child and the Three Kings at Christmas and Christ's passion during Lent. I encourage my Facebook Friends to think about what they see. Always the professor! The exhibits are in public places. I love the thought of a photograph of Christ at the Pillar, a crucifix or the nave of a cathedral displayed in a public library or city hall. I've come to think of myself as a photo-evangelist. There's no such word in spell check, yet.

It was easiest for the Lord to call me through my mind, my intellect. As a professor, I've spent most of my life in my head. It took more effort to get to my heart. The Lord broke through to my heart in the Holy Land. I went to the Holy Land in 2015 with Terra Sancta Pilgrimages, a Franciscan group. The Franciscans have custody of the shrines in the Holy Land. They are in charge of the sacred places. We had access to people and places the average tourist would never see. We spent some time in the desert near Bethlehem where the Lord first touched my heart.

Cathedral of Wertheimer, Germany

The desert was harsh and forbidding. There was nothing there but the long road back to civilization. There were no shops or gas stations, only a souvenir peddler and his camel. The desert has a long history in the Bible as a place for spiritual enlightenment and purification. The Israelites wandered in the desert for forty years before entering the Promised Land. It was a heavy penance to pay for backsliding and worshiping the golden calf after they crossed the Red Sea. John the Baptist worked in a similar environment when he was a voice "crying in the wilderness". He preached the coming of the messiah and urged people to repent of their sins. Jesus was baptized by John and then went to the desert to pray and fast for 40 days. There the devil tempted Jesus with riches, power and comfort. The desert fathers, holy men in the first centuries after Christ, lived in the desert of northern Africa. They lived free of all attachments in an effort to emulate Jesus and to draw closer to the Lord.

Our pilgrim group went out to the desert in Wadi Qelt, not far from Bethlehem. I looked forward to the solitude and silence I would find there. I had visions of praying like the hermits, the desert fathers and mothers from the earliest days of Christianity. The members of our pilgrim group spread out on a ridge overlooking the vast emptiness. A terrible fear descended on me. I'm not afraid of heights. I've explored Machu Picchu and stood on the rim of the Grand Canyon. This was no more than a hill overlooking the desert. I was surprised by the effect on me. I was scared to death.

A terrible sense of dread descended upon me. I stayed glued to my rocky seat, too terrified to move. I didn't know what was happening to me. I was relieved when I saw the pilgrims walking back to the bus. My ordeal was over. I was able to get five minutes of spiritual direction at the next rest stop. We came to the conclusions that I hadn't developed a fear of heights. It was an internal fear. I had come face to face with my fear of getting close to Jesus. There was nothing to distract me in the desert. Nothing interrupted my communion with the Lord and it was terrifying. I know my fear of moving closer to the Lord was a reaction to being married. The more I gave to my husband, the less I had of myself. I was afraid of getting lost in a relationship again.

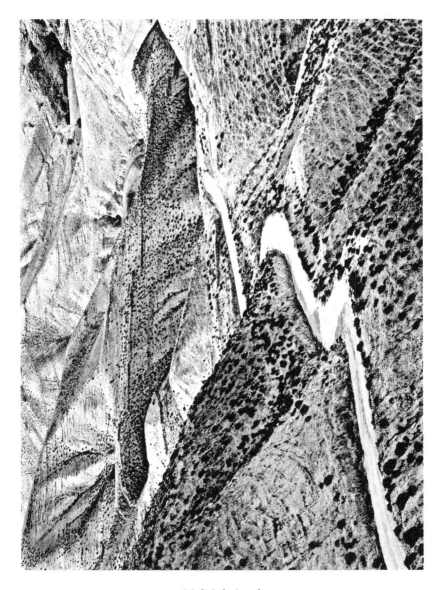

Wadi Qelt, Israel

I talked about my fear of moving closer to Jesus with my spiritual director years later. He told me to take it to the Blessed Mother. I sat in the walk-in tabernacle where I lived and thought about my experience in the desert. I was afraid of losing myself, of annihilation of the self. I feared that if I got too close to the Lord, I would be assumed into the mystical body of Christ and no longer exist. The unitive experience that mystics seek is a gift of God, not something you can bring on my by yourself. Regardless, the thought terrified me.

I imagined talking with the Blessed Mother. I saw her as an actress from the TV movie about the life of Christ. She didn't look like the beautiful young woman of the statues and holy cards. She looked like a middle-aged woman in peasant garb, like a real woman from that time. She was angry and raised her finger to scold me. She said, "Don't be afraid of my son. Don't be afraid to go to Jesus." Jesus joined the conversation and said, "Chris, I put an adoration chapel in your house, why don't you come to see me more often?" What could I say?

I had had my first successive locution. St. John of the Cross defined it as a voice in your head that comes from meditation. It's much different from a natural locution that comes from outside your head. That would really freak me out. The Blessed Mother told me not to be afraid of her son and Jesus told me to visit him more often. My fear of the annihilation of myself disappeared instantly and I started to visit Jesus more often. The Lord had touched my heart. I wonder what my reaction to prayer in the Wadi Qelt would be today. I hope I get the chance to visit that spot again and experience peace rather than fear.

We went to the Mount of Olives soon after our visit to the desert. It proved to be a healing experience, and very restorative compared to my time in the desert. It was just what I needed. We spent an entire afternoon at the Franciscan retreat site. We were in an olive grove across from the Old City of Jerusalem. We could see thousands of Jewish graves and the Golden Door through which the Messiah will enter when he returns. We had a simple lunch and the opportunity to go to confession. I hadn't planned it, but was the first one to ask for the forgiveness of my sins. That gave me the rest of the afternoon for prayer and, of course, photographs.

We walked down the slope of the Mount of Olives and heard Mass at the Church of the Agony. Many of you are familiar with the picture of Jesus praying on a rock in the Mount of Olives before he is arrested. He asks his Father "If you are willing, take this cup away from me; still, not my will but yours be done." Jesus was in agony knowing what was about to happen to him. I had been in agony in the desert and was feeling revived after my time on the Mount of Olives. I soon learned that the Lord wasn't through reaching into my heart yet.

I had prayed to be open to the Holy Spirit before I went on the pilgrimage, but didn't expect Him to be so hard on me. Near the end of the pilgrimage, we visited Cana, the site of Jesus' first miracle at the wedding feast. Apparently, the hosts were running low on wine. Mary learned of the problem and asked Jesus to do something. She knew he could work miracles although he had yet to perform one in public. He asked for large jars to be filled with water and told the steward to take some of the wine to the chief steward. The wine He produced was the best served that night. The Miracle at Cana has continued to be associated with marriage. Several of the married couples in our group were going to renew their vows in the chapel said to be over the room where Jesus performed the miracle. We planned to purchase Cana Wedding Wine in the shop across from the chapel to continue the celebration.

We went to Cana on October 17th, what would have been my 34th wedding anniversary. What a coincidence. I had been divorced for over twenty years and my ex-husband had died the previous year. There hadn't been any relationship in decades. We hadn't spoken since we signed our last joint IRS return. Our group went to lunch before our visit to the chapel. We were told to be sure and look up to the ceiling when we entered the restaurant. There would be something really interesting to see. It was a life-sized motorcycle made of rattan. My ex-husband had been a motorcycle police officer. Another coincidence? So, there I was in Cana on my wedding anniversary and a life-sized Harley was hanging in the restaurant. Just a coincidence or was I in for something?

We climbed the hill to the chapel and I told our priest about the amazing coincidences. I could feel the tears starting to form in my eyes. I took a collection for the use of the chapel, my usual duty, and left. I dissolved in tears by the time I reached the marble steps outside of the chapel. I was overwhelmed with sorrow. I sobbed, great belly busting sobs. I wept like I've never wept before. The sobs kept coming for the next 30 minutes. Other tourist groups passed by and I kept sobbing. I cried for my failed marriage. It was never blessed by the Church and was considered a fornicated relationship. I cried for all my sins against the Sacrament of Matrimony. Eventually a friend came out of the chapel and literally held me together. I managed to get back to the bus. I was spent. It took a long time to process what had happened and I was grateful to be left alone for the bus ride to our next stop.

I wasn't accustomed to such emotional outbursts. I'm an academic, a scholar. I live in my head. A psychologist stays in control while others fall apart in her office. God broke through to my heart in very dramatic ways during my pilgrimage to the Holy Land. I wasn't expecting drama, to be blown away like that. All of my emotional experiences during my pilgrimage to the Holy Land couldn't be just coincidences. They were too personal. They were too powerful. I asked to be open to the Holy Spirit and I received more than I ever expected.

Over time, the Lord touched my heart with more emotions than fear and sorrow. I came to feel that Jesus loved me, loved me as an individual. I learned the song, "Jesus Loves You," as a little child. I thought of it in terms of the plural "you". Jesus loves all of his children. I had difficulty understanding how he could love me in particular. One day I was praying in front of a statue of the Sacred Heart at St. Anne de Detroit, the oldest parish in Detroit, Michigan. It is a very common image in Catholic churches. The statue in St. Anne de Detroit was very ordinary. Nothing unusual had ever been attributed to it. It didn't speak to me that day or produce a miracle worth mentioning either. But it was the first time I felt that Jesus loved me, Christine Panyard as an individual. He loved me not as one of the many members of his Church, but as a being separate from any of his other children. Jesus loved me. Maybe that realization was a miracle of sorts.

The emotional experience of being loved by Jesus changed my relationship to Him. I felt closer to the Lord and wanted to spend more time with Him. I started going to church more often until I was going daily. When I'm traveling with a group or the weather keeps me at home, I read the Mass. My spiritual director described that as a spiritual communion. It's not the same as attending Mass, but it helps to maintain my connection with the Lord. At Jesus' suggestion, I visit Him more often in the walk-in tabernacle where I live. I don't go every day. I guess that fear of getting too close is still operating, but I wouldn't be surprised if eventually I start going daily.

Chapel at Cana, Galilee

Feeling loved by Jesus has made me want to share my gifts with others. Slowly, I'm developing the courage to speak more freely of my faith and the many blessings I have received. I gave three presentations at St. Mary of the Snow, my church in Milford, Michigan. I was preaching to the choir but it was a good place to begin. I was sharing my experience of Renaissance art and scripture with interested Catholics. In a sense, I was testing the waters. Several years later I gave a presentation about my pilgrimage to the Holy Land. I was still being very academic, not quite ready to talk about my spiritual gifts.

Every year we have a walking challenge during Lent at the retirement community where I live. We've walked to Jerusalem and followed the footsteps of Christ. The goal is to accumulate enough steps as a community to make the trips. The wrap-up for the last challenge was my presentation on Gothic cathedrals. I began in the square in front of the cathedral, walked around the cathedral and finally entered it. I took the audience up the naïve and down the aisles. We walked around the ambulatories and towards the altar. You've already seen most of the photographs that were in my power point presentation.

This time I was different. The academic had faded into the background and the photo evangelist started to emerge. This time I wasn't afraid to share what really happened to me on my trips. I felt safe and talked about the gifts from the Holy Spirit I had received along the way. And guess what happened? The audience loved it. No one laughed at me or ran out of the chapel in horror. I wasn't talking about my crazy, strange, bizarre experiences. I was sharing my gifts from the Holy Spirit.

The Christian Women's Guild at Henry Ford Village invited me to give a talk at their annual Christmas Dinner. The majority of the members were Protestant. Catholics weren't even allowed to join until recently. I was dumbfounded to learn that some Protestant groups don't even believe that Catholics are Christian. Many in the group had heard me speak before and certainly knew me from the dining room and the hallways at our retirement community. I was a known quantity, so my religion wasn't an issue. The theme of the event was Heaven on Earth. How could I tackle such an immense subject in the fifteen minutes I was allotted?

I decided to talk about heaven on earth as moments when we encounter the Divine, moments when we feel the presence of God. I took a deep breath and began. I spoke about encountering God in majestic, larger than life experiences. I went to the Grand Canyon the previous summer and was blest to be able to stay on the North Rim. Our cabin was fifty yards from the edge. I eased out before dawn to position myself for some great photographs. People came in their pajamas, carrying steaming cups of coffee. Children were laughing and everyone was enjoying their good fortune to be in such a magical place. A hush fell over the crowd as the day began to break. The sun rose over the edge of the canyon and as it became more visible the crowd became still. Only the sound of the breeze rustling some nearby trees and the song of a bird greeting the day broke the silence. The Grand Canyon became a cathedral. Everyone felt the awesome presence of God. Light fell across the canyon as if someone had lifted a window shade. The experience of God lighting the Grand Canyon was breathtaking. The crowd, now a congregation, felt the majesty of God the Creator, King of the Universe.

We experience the presence of God in quiet moments with the people we love. Holding a newborn infant, enjoying her warmth, softness and the smell of her skin are encounters with God. Looking into the eyes of a loved one at a special time in their lives or holding the hand of a parent as they slip into death are God moments.

We also experience the presence of God, experience heaven on earth, in quiet moments alone with God. I experience those moments after receiving Holy Communion. I sit at the front of the church so I can be among the first people to receive both the body and blood of Jesus. I'm able to return to my seat with the maximum time left for prayer before the priest gives the final blessing and we stand to sing the recessional hymn. I feel God is with me as the Holy Eucharist moves down my throat. Somehow, my prayers seem stronger, more potent during those fifteen or so minutes. I don't sing the Communion hymn and am not aware of the other members of the congregation streaming past me. Sometimes I'm surprised to find the priest has finished his housekeeping duties before I finish my prayer. I can only describe it as a turning in on myself and feeling the presence of God.

Sacred Heart of Jesus, St. Anne de Detroit

I say this prayer after receiving the Eucharist:

Lord Jesus, open my mind. Lord, open my mind.
Lord Jesus, open my heart. Lord, open my heart.
Lord Jesus, open my hands, Lord, open my hands.
Lord Jesus, open my life. Lord, open my life.
Lord Jesus, open my soul. Lord, open my soul.

Lord Jesus, open my mind, my heart, my hands, my life and my soul.
Lord fill me with your Holy Spirit.
Lord Jesus, open me to your will. Lord, open me to your will.

This prayer didn't come to me all at once. It came line by line. I wrote it down in the order in which it came. Reflecting on it, the prayer came in the order in which God had spoken to me, the order in which God touched me. God came to me first through my mind. The Lord touched this professor through her intellect. My passion to learn all I could about Renaissance art, artists and cathedrals kept me in museums, libraries and bookstores. More importantly, I stayed in the presence of the Blessed Sacrament in the cathedrals and churches I visited, which moved me back to Church.

God touched my heart in many ways during my journey back to Church. He opened me emotionally and made me feel intense fear, sorrow, and joy. The academic who lived in her head found herself clinging for life on a precipice in the desert and weeping in the streets of Cana. The psychologist who remained in control while other people fell apart in her office was falling apart in public. Emotions were sharing the stage with intellect. I was becoming a more balanced person.

The Lord touched my hands and made me productive. He's kept my hands very busy, especially for a retired person. I wrote seven books. Not all have been or ever will be published. Some had value only as training exercises for my new work. I've done six different presentations where I had the opportunity to use the teaching-skills I honed at the University of Detroit Mercy. I've won ten awards for my photography in the three years since I began exhibiting my work. My professional skills have been used at Henry Ford Village to coordinate the application for the Pinnacle Award. It is given to the retirement community that best exemplifies the seven pillars of wellness which include the areas of social, emotional, vocational, physical, spiritual, environmental and intellectual well-being. Henry Ford Village came in second out of over one hundred communities in 2017. I organized and implemented an Art Walk to keep residents moving during the Michigan's cold winter. It was more successful than I could have ever imagined. The Lord seems to like my work and continues to send me projects that enable me to be useful. My life has opened up in ways I could never have imagined since coming back to the Lord.

Where do I go from here? I can't begin to imagine where the Lord will take me next. What I've done and accomplished in the past ten years amazes me. I hope to continue traveling, taking photographs, writing and sharing the Lord with others. I know that my capacity for that kind of life can change at any moment and hope to make the most of the good health the Lord has given me. I want to be useful to His plan and to his Church. I would like to be able to use the skills He has given me to lead people to experience joy in the Lord. My life is open to work for Him as He sees fit not as I would like. I'm excited and at peace that it will it be His will, not mine, which will be done.

11

LORD, OPEN MY LIFE

THE Holy Spirit started nudging me again and I decided to re-read St. Teresa of Avila's famous book *Interior Castles*. I read her work for the first time more than twenty years ago and found it daunting. She wrote of hearing voices, locutions, visions, and ecstasy. St. Teresa was very difficult to understand and hard to accept given my training as a behavioral scientist. To be blunt, I thought she needed a psychologist more than I needed a mystic. I re-read her work shortly before visiting Avila. I had made some progress in my own spiritual development by then and had some of the same experiences she reported. I wanted to see how I would experience her work this time around. Wonder of wonders! I loved it. St. Teresa no longer needed a therapist. Her words moved me. I felt the need to meditate on St. Teresa's work and produced a devotional booklet for personal prayer and reflection. I underlined passages in *Interior Castle* as I went along and collected those that were meaningful to me. I organized this collection according to the rooms one visited during the journey through the castle. This format allowed me to access her work more easily and helped me to keep track of my own spiritual journey.

I went to Spain with a tour group and decided to stay in Madrid for a few extra days. It was a very difficult trip. I had a minor hamstring injury just before the trip. It was noticeable when I walked, but nothing that would keep me from marching through Spain. Three weeks of trekking on cobblestones, hoofing up and down medieval hill towns, and walking on concrete city streets took their toll. I had developed severe tendonitis in both legs.

By the end of the trip every step was agony, but I was not going to stop. I planned a day trip to Avila and Segovia, beautiful hill top towns an hour outside of Madrid, and, by golly, I was going to complete it.

St. Teresa of Avila and St. John of the Cross were two of Avila's most famous residents. They worked together and were involved in the Counter Reformation of the Catholic Church. The lifestyle in the 16th Century Carmelite monasteries and convents had become lax. They were no longer austere, enclosed communities for a pious few. In a sense, they became social centers and men and women not part of the Carmelite community visited regularly. St. Teresa spent twenty years in that sort of community before she decided that a change was needed. She and St. John of the Cross founded new religious houses that were based on the original, stricter Rule of St. Albert from the 13th Century. Monks and nuns moved into small communities of thirteen residents. Socializing with the neighbors was strictly regulated and the enclosed religious men and women maintained a contemplative life of prayer. These new communities were called Discalced Carmelites which means shoeless. They adopted sandals as the preferred footwear as the weather allowed. The Discalced Carmelites were distinguished from the older order by their piety and fashion.

St. Teresa of Avila and St. John of the Cross put the proscription for a contemplative life into words, and with the advent of the printing press, made it available to others beyond the walls of their foundations. Their books were much more than "how to" manuals. They were gifted writers who were able to put the contemplative experience, the experience of union with God and the pain of absence from of God into words. Their writings earned them the titles of Doctor of the Church and have become the foundational works of the Discalced Carmelites.

It's hard to imagine, but the tendonitis in my legs caused me to stop after the morning visit to Avila. I was in no shape to make it to the top of another hill town. I'd visit St. John of the Cross another time. All I wanted to do was sit on the bus and wait for the ride back to my hotel. We arrived in Segovia, the burial place of St. John of the Cross, in time for lunch. I explained my predicament to the tour guide. She told me to walk up the next hill and take a taxi back to Madrid. She waved me off vaguely to where the bus would be and went to lunch. An Argentinian on the trip told her I needed better directions and the tour guide was miffed that I was interfering with her free time. Finally, she came out and gave me better directions to the bus parking lot. In all my years of traveling the world, I had never been treated me so rudely by a tour guide. Usually, they do everything possible to help their charges. She was not behaving like a good shepherd and I got a complete refund for the trip when I returned home.

I was angry, hurt and very upset. I was also very hungry. I couldn't stomach having lunch in the same establishment as our tour guide so I limped to a restaurant frequented by locals and then to the bus stop. The bus stop was a vacant lot with no shelter or benches. I found a large rock and sat there for at least an hour and a half. The tour of Spain had been fascinating. We went from Barcelona to Gibraltar, through Portugal with a rest stop in Fatima and on to Madrid. This was a tour and not a pilgrimage so there was no time allocated for prayer. I pulled out the rosary I always carry and prayed. Although very uncomfortable, it was the only prayerful moments I had during that trip.

I took as many photographs of Avila as I could take while I hobbled through the streets. I had more than enough to illustrate my devotional book based on *Interior Castle*. The book became a present to my spiritual director on the 25th anniversary of this ordination to the priesthood. We both find it useful so I sent a book proposal to the Institute of Carmelite Studies hoping they would share our assessment. The ICS requested a copy of the manuscript, always a good sign. I hoped *Essential Interior Castle* would become my second book. I trusted that if God found it useful, it would be published.

The second nudge came in September 2017. I went on a tour of historic churches in Michigan's Upper Peninsula with a group called Prayer Pilgrimages. The U.P. is home to copper and iron mines, hunting grounds and thousands of square miles of forests. The end of the 19th century and beginning of the 20th century were boom times for the mining and lumber companies that developed the region. Those businesses declined dramatically in modern times and left the U.P. more desolate than the Michigan on the other side of the Straits of Mackinaw. Unemployment was very high. Iron Mountain and Copper Harbor became tourist areas rather than industrial centers. What a surprise to find grand neo-Gothic cathedrals there. The boom times brought immigrants from all over Europe. The same immigrant groups who came to Detroit to work in the auto factories went to the U.P. for the good paying jobs in the mines and lumber mills. They brought their faith with them and built beautiful churches as the centers of their new communities.

St. John of the Cross and St. Teresa of Avila, Convento de St. Teresa de Avila, Avila, Spain

Our last stop on this pilgrimage was the Carmelite Monastery of the Holy Cross in Iron Mountain, Michigan. It was a Discalced Carmelite Monastery. I hadn't planned it, but there I was with St. Teresa's sisters. We had the opportunity to spend some time with the enclosed nuns. They sat behind a screen in a small parlor. I was one of the last of our group to enter the room and all the seats were taken. That was OK. I could stand for our short visit. Fr. Portelli, the pilgrimage chaplain, gave me his seat directly across the screen from the Mother Prioress. The pious women we met left the world and will spend their entire life in an enclosed community following a rule established centuries ago. This was a new experience for me and the first time most of us had encountered cloistered nuns.

The nuns of the Monastery of the Holy Cross graciously answered our questions about their lifestyle and the challenges they face as enclosed nuns today. When we got up to leave, I told the Mother Prioress about my experience in Avila and my prayer book. She said, "You have the aura of St. Teresa about you." I was stunned. How could anyone say such a thing about me, let alone the Prioress of a Carmelite Monastery? What did she see in me? What did she feel? There was no time to pursue her strange remark. I floated off to Mass and could hardly contain my amazement and joy. I've described my encounters with the Divine or mystical experiences several times before as "floating". My feet are always firmly planted on the ground. No levitation is occurring. But there is the sense of being lifted up. Maybe uplifted is what I really mean.

I shared this experience with my spiritual director and then came the third nudge. He suggested that I explore the Secular Carmelites. Secular Carmelite? I was familiar with the Third Order Franciscans, but Carmelites. How could an enclosed order have a secular branch? Google to the rescue! I learned that many orders have three divisions, friars or priests, nuns and laity respectively, the first, second and third orders. Secular orders are open to men and women, single and married. The only requirement to begin the process of entering a secular order is to be a practicing Catholics and to be seeking a way to serve God. Every order has its own charism, a special gift from the Holy Spirit for the good of the Church. Franciscans are noted for their service to the poor, Jesuits for their work as scholars. Discalced Carmelites are noted for their lives of prayer. They seek to share the spirituality of St. Teresa of Avila and St. John of the Cross with the world. Their focus is on prayer, meditation, contemplation and the sacraments as they move towards a greater union with God. My spiritual director's suggestion was right on target. The Secular Discalced Carmelites appealed to me and represented a way of life worth exploring.

I've mentioned "spiritual director" several times and feel like I need a short digression to explain it more fully. St. Teresa wrote in her autobiography: "The beginner (in spiritual development) requires advice, so that he may see where his greatest benefit lies. To this end a director is most necessary." From the vantage point of having practiced psychology for 43 years, I see spiritual direction as psychotherapy for the soul. A spiritual director works to help an individual develop a more satisfying and effective spiritual life. Spiritual direction is working on the relationship between an individual and God. It is very different in focus from reducing pathology and improving functioning in this world, but the techniques are very similar.

I continue meet with Fr. James Bilot, the pastor of St Paul on the Lake in Grosse Pointe Farms MI, every other month. He had years of experience as a spiritual director and worked with seminarians as well as parishioners. I learned useful things from his homilies so thought he might be useful to me as a spiritual director as well. Fr. Jim operates in a very non-directive manner. He would be considered a client-centered or Rogerian practitioner in my business. We talk about my relationship with God. Am I moving closer to God? What are some of the impediments or sticking points in our relationship? How is my new spirituality affecting the rest of my life and how is my life affecting my new spirituality? It's an opportunity to discuss what's moving in my spirit with someone who is non-judgmental. Fr. Jim doesn't tell me what to do or how to be in a relationship with God, although occasionally he does nudge me. He validates what is happening to me and provides a safe place to explore this part of my being. He's helped me to understand my experience from a spiritual perspective rather than a psychological/scientific one. I no longer wonder if I'm going crazy. I've bravely opened myself up to the Lord and now feel comfortable with the Holy Spirit moving in my life. Fr. Jim provides light and support for my journey.

I followed up on my spiritual director's suggestion to explore the Secular Carmelites. I learned that the Carmelites traced their origins to the Prophet Elijah, were recognized by Rome in the Thirteenth Century and had monasteries and secular communities all over the world. Eight Discalced Carmelite Monasteries and sixteen secular communities were located in Michigan. I found the Assumption of the Blessed Virgin Mary Community of Secular Discalced Carmelites at a church in Detroit, just twenty minutes from my home. Their location and meeting times fit my needs perfectly. Nudge four?

I went to my first meeting in December 2017. The church was built in the 1920's and is a hodgepodge of styles. Overall, it has the feel of a medieval church. Large limestone blocks rise to a painted wooden ceiling. It is dark and cool, just my style. The parish is "traditional". The altar is against the wall rather that facing the congregation. Mass is frequently said in Latin and only males function as altar servers. The first meeting I attended was a silent day of reflection, not their typical monthly community meeting. The day started with a Tridentine Mass (formal Latin Mass), rosary and morning prayers in church. Fr. Perrone, the community's spiritual assistant, gave three short talks followed by quiet reflection. There was time for socializing and I found the community to be warm and welcoming. It was a wonderful introduction to the Secular Discalced Carmelites and I decided to return the following month.

I am discerning, deciding with the help of God and the Carmelite community, if I should begin the formation process to become a Secular Carmelite. I won't be entering a convent or wearing a habit. Secular Carmelites live as married or single men and women, work at a variety of careers and are fully engaged in the world. Their lives are infused with the spirit and practice of Carmelite spirituality. This means that they are practicing Catholics who spend more time than the average Catholic in prayer and study. The purpose of formation is "to prepare the person to live the charism and spirituality of Carmel in its following of Christ and in service to its mission". Preparation includes inspiration by the Holy Spirit to live in accord with the principles of Carmelite spirituality. St. Teresa of Avila and St. John of the Cross are the spiritual parents of the Discalced Carmelites. Formation involves studying their work as well as learning their style of prayer and the Divine Office. I can hardly believe I am writing this. Ten years ago, I could never have imagined I would ever consider joining a religious community. Now I'm discerning if religious life is for me and if I want to begin a six-year formation program to become a Secular Discalced Carmelite. I would probably be the world's oldest novice! By the time I would be eligible to make definitive promises and become a fully professed member of the order, I would be seventy-six years old.

The formation period has three phases. Aspirancy is the first phase and lasts approximately one year. It is preparation for the reception of the ceremonial Brown Scapular. The first Carmelites lived on Mt. Carmel in

Israel during the 12th Century. They were forced to leave because of the spread of Islam in the region and relocated to Europe where the order continued to face persecution. St. Simon was praying to the Blessed Virgin in a convent at Cambridge, England when she appeared to him. She gave him a loose garment worn over the shoulders, hence the name scapula, on both the front and back of the habit. It was coarse brown cloth and hung to the knees. It was a sign of privileges from the Blessed Mother and said to preserve those wearing it at the time of death from damnation. Many miracles have been associated with the scapula. Monks and nuns in enclosed communities wear a similar garment over their habit. A smaller version, a ten-inch square, is used when an individual is admitted into formation towards the temporary and definitive promises of a Secular Carmelite. It is worn during community meetings. A smaller version may be worn all the time or a scapular medal can be worn in its place. Scapulae and scapular medals are very common symbols of devotion to the Blessed Virgin and are worn by many Catholics outside of the Carmelites.

The next two phases lead to the Temporary Promises (two years) and the Definitive Promises (three years). During these periods the candidate follows a proscribed curriculum covering the works of principle Carmelite saints. The works of St. Teresa of Avila, St. John of the Cross, St. Therese of Lisieux, and St. Edith Stein have been so valued by the Catholic Church that those saints have been declared Doctors of the Church. It is an honor shared by the likes of St. Augustine and St. Thomas Aquinas. Individuals in formation take part in community activities, rituals and services throughout formation. The decision to become a full-fledged Secular Discalced Carmelite is a mutual decision between the individual and the community. The Carmelites must want me as much as I want them.

My journey to the Church had been very long. It started with my baptism in 1947 and seventy years later I was contemplating joining a religious community. At my parent's insistence, I went to church and received the sacraments. I was raised Catholic, but not very Catholic. I left the church shortly after my parents said going was my choice. I spent a good many years wandering around outside of the Church. I didn't attend Mass and certainly was not scrupulous about following the Ten Commandments let alone the precepts of the Church.

My intellectual curiosity, appreciation of art, and obsession with Michelangelo led me to the front door of many churches. I spent ten years studying art and taking photographs in cathedrals around the world. I never thought about being in the presence of the Blessed Sacrament, being in the presence of the Lord. I was unaware that anything was happening to me during all those hours spent searching for the roots of Michelangelo's greatness or setting up the next award-winning photo. I was transformed by the stimuli coming from my surroundings. Being in the presence of the Blessed Sacrament amidst beautiful art and architecture in Gothic and Renaissance cathedrals changed me in ways I could have never predicted. My spiritual director said that God duped me. All that time I thought I was studying Renaissance Art, God was slowly reeling me in to Himself. I went from being a lapsed Catholic to exploring the possibility of entering a religious community.

I had what I thought were strange, weird, and crazy experiences in churches, especially Gothic cathedrals. Then I learned to think of them as remarkable coincidences. Now I accept them as gifts from the Holy Spirit. There were too many wonderful incidents in churches that could only be explained as the movement of the Lord in my life. It's amazing to think how different the outcome would have been if I had sought psychiatric help rather than spiritual direction. I've learned that I am not crazy. I've been deluged with blessings. The Lord has given me many skills and experiences to draw from as I continue my "perfecting journey". I hope to use writing and photography to nudge others on their journeys. The Lord has opened my life in so many ways and has helped me walk towards His altar. I hope my work brings a soul or two with me.

The Holy Spirit, St. Mary, Our Lady of the Annunciation Church, Rockwood, MI

WORKS CONSULTED

Creighton-Jobe, Reverend Ronald, ed. *The Illustrated Encyclopedia of Catholicism*, London: Lorenz Books an imprint of Anness Publishing Ltd, 2009.

Cook, William R. *The Cathedral Course Guidebook*, Chantilly, VA, 2010.

King, Ross. *Michelangelo and the Pope's Ceiling*, New York: Penguin Books, 2003

Symonds, John Addington. *The Life of Michelangelo Buonarroti*. Philadelphia: University of Pennsylvania Press, 2002. Originally published by J.C. Nimmo and Charles Scribner's Sons, 1911.

Voragine, Jacobus de. *The Golden Legend Readings on the Saints*, Princeton: Princeton University Press, 1993.

Wallace, William E. *Michelangelo: The Complete Sculpture, Painting, Architecture*. New York: Hugh Lauter Leven Associates, Inc., 1998.

Made in the USA
Middletown, DE
18 August 2022

71666843R00070